mom ♥ me
& me
knits

mom & me knits

20 PRETTY PROJECTS FOR MOTHERS AND DAUGHTERS

by **Stefanie Japel**

photographs by **Aimée Herring**

CHRONICLE BOOKS
SAN FRANCISCO

Library of Congress Cataloging-in-Publication Data:
Japel, Stefanie.
  Mom & me knits : 20 pretty projects for mothers and daughters / Stefanie Japel
     p. cm.
   ISBN 978-0-8118-7929-3 (hardcover)
   1. Knitting—Patterns. 2. Women's clothing. I. Title.
 TT825.J388 2012
 746.43'2041—dc22

                                         2011011416

Manufactured in China

Designed by *Emily Dubin*
Photo styling by *Marie Moss*

10 9 8 7 6 5 4 3 2 1

Chronicle Books LLC
680 Second Street
San Francisco, California 94107
www.chroniclebooks.com

ACKNOWLEDGMENTS

For their undying support through the production of this book, I would like to thank my family. Sorry about all of the late nights, guys!

I also thank the featured companies for generously supplying the yarns for these projects, and I doubly thank Knit Picks for also supplying needles and accessories.

My heartfelt thanks to Jodi Warshaw for approaching me to do this book at the perfect time in my life, when I have the perfect inspiration, and I extend my gratitude to my agent, Judy Heiblum, for making sure that it all came together.

*This book is dedicated
to Mazie and Olive Japel,
who are my inspiration.*

Contents

Introduction

I love designing patterns. I'm best known for creating seamless garments that fit and flatter women's figures. I've written two books on the subject, and I've even appeared on TV's *Knitty Gritty* to discuss my design style. When my daughters were born, I was faced with a new knitting challenge: create children's garments that appeal to both parents and children—and feel and fit great. I'm not a fluffy-pink person, and my daughters (so far) aren't fluffy-pink people, either. This poses a bit of a problem when I'm trying to find clothes for them: if you walk into the children's clothing section at any department store, it's clear that Girls Wear Pink. It's even hard to find knitting patterns for girls that aren't saccharine-sweet confections. Not long after my first daughter was born, I started publishing knitting patterns for children. I like to create cute garments, but ones that aren't traditionally "girly." I'm aiming to make clothes that aren't all pink, don't all have lace or ruffles, and can be worn all the time, not just for dressy occasions. For each pattern that I've designed for kids, I've received hundreds of e-mail messages requesting the pattern for adults!

In this book, I combine my love of women's designs and my desire to create cute, sophisticated-yet-casual clothing for girls by offering a collection of mother-and-daughter knits. In the following pages, you'll find one-piece garments, knit from the top down, for little girls and their moms (or aunts, grandmas, or family friends). I didn't want the knits to be too matchy-matchy. Instead, I created patterns where the adult pattern is more sophisticated and the child's pattern is a playful, youthful version of it. Some simply coordinate due to shared stitch patterns or use of the same yarn. Other sets started with the infant sweater, with the adult sweater following as a companion piece. Still others started with the adult sweater and were sized down.

While all of the garments are constructed from the top down on circular needles, each presents the knitter with an opportunity to do something a little bit different—and maybe even learn something new. In making the Puebla Tops, for example, you'll do a little bit of duplicate stitch and surface embroidery. For the Library Cardigans, you'll "knit on" little I-cord button loops. The Aran Coats are shaped using increases inside the cabled sections. I hope that you'll enjoy learning how to create these little details and that you will find ways to use them again in your knitting.

I've included patterns sized for infants (or child) through adult, most up to a 50-in/127-cm or larger bust measurement. All of the sweaters fit well and are designed with care for real women and the little girls they love.

Your Knitting Basket

The majority of the garments in this book are knit at least partially in the round. To knit them, you'll need circular needles. If you plan to knit a lot of patterns in the round, I recommend that you invest in a nice set of circular needles with interchangeable tips, like the sets from Denise Needle, Addi, or Knit Picks. This way, you'll always have the correct needle size and cable length. If you are just starting out knitting in the round and aren't sure if you want to invest in a set, you can just buy individual needles as you need them, and it will only be a matter of time before you've built up a nice collection of needle sizes and lengths.

You will also need a few other items for the patterns in this book:

TOOLS

Darning needle or tapestry needle

Measuring tape

Scissors

Stitch holders or lengths of waste yarn

Stitch markers

YARNS

The yarns used for the projects in this book are only suggestions. Please feel free to substitute yarn from your own stash for any of the yarns in these patterns. However, if you do substitute, please be sure to swatch and see that your gauge is the same as that called for in the pattern. If you don't swatch, you will not achieve the desired size, drape, or fit in the finished garment. Please also be sure to substitute a yarn of similar fiber composition. These yarns have been selected because they achieve a certain look, feel, and drape in the finished garment. Substituting yarns with different properties and compositions will create fabrics that differ in quality from those pictured in this book.

Techniques

The patterns in this book assume a basic level of knitting know-how. In this section, you will find detailed instructions for some of the more involved processes in this book.

PICOT BIND-OFF
(Used in Puebla Top and Ladylike Cardigan)

This is a decorative bind-off technique in which you not only bind off the last row of knitting but also create a decorative edging by adding and then immediately binding off extra stitches.

To work this bind-off: Bind off 3 sts, *cast on 3 sts using knit-on cast-on method, bind off 5 sts; repeat from * around, bind off remaining sts.

BACKWARD LOOP CAST-ON METHOD
(Can use in all projects for buttonholes or at underarms)

This is a quick way to cast on a few stitches in the middle of a row when working buttonholes.

To work this cast-on method: With work in the right hand, and working yarn in the left hand, use the working yarn to create a loop around the left thumb. Twist the loop once and place on the right-hand needle. Repeat until you've cast on as many stitches as called for in the pattern.

KNIT-ON CAST-ON METHOD
(Used in larger sizes of all garments at underarm)

While this cast-on method can be used to cast on all of the stitches for a project, it is especially useful for casting on stitches in the middle of a row, such as when working buttonholes or casting on stitches at underarm in top-down sweaters.

To work this cast-on method: Insert right-hand needle into the first stitch on the left-hand needle as if to knit. Knit one stitch, but don't slip the stitch off. Instead, transfer the new stitch (the one on the right-hand needle) onto the left-hand needle. Repeat until you've "knit on" as many stitches as called for in the pattern.

BUTTONHOLES
(Used in Library Cardigan, Aran Coat, Lace Cardigan, Classic Cardigan, and Ladylike Cardigan)

One-stitch buttonhole: Row 1: Yo, k2tog. Row 2: Work in pattern stitch (knit, purl, seed st, etc.).

Two-stitch buttonhole: Row 1: BO 2 sts. Row 2: Work in patt st to bound-off sts; using the "knitting on" method, CO 2 sts.

Three-stitch buttonhole: Row 1: BO 3 sts. Row 2: Work in patt st to bound-off sts; using the "knitting on" method, CO 3 sts.

SPACING BUTTONHOLES EVENLY
(Used in Classic Cardigan and Ladylike Cardigan)

Using this method, you will be able to place buttonholes evenly along a front band, regardless of the number of stitches on the needle or the number of buttons to be placed.

As an example, let's say that you have 70 stitches for your button band and need to place 8 buttons. The first thing you need to do is to space the buttons evenly on one side of the band and figure out how to space the buttonholes. Start by placing a button at one end of the button band, and another button at the other end, 3 stitches from the edge. (The distance from the edge will depend on the size of your buttons; you want the button to sit right on the band but not overlap the top or bottom edge.) Now, you need to place the remaining 6 buttons evenly over the remaining 64 stitches. Divide the remaining 64 stitches into 6 sections of 9 stitches each plus one more section with 10 stitches. Center each buttonhole about every 9 (or 10) stitches, and mark the spot with a pin or removable stitch marker.

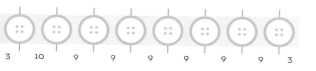

At this point, you've placed your buttons, but you still need to figure out how to work the buttonholes.

First, check the pattern to see how large the buttonholes should be. Typical buttonhole sizes are one stitch, two stitch, or three stitch. One-stitch buttonholes are easy to work: simply knit to the point where the button is placed (work to the pin or marker) and work a "yo, k2tog" combination, and do the same to the end of the buttonhole row of the band.

Two-stitch buttonholes are worked in a similar manner, but you need to be a little bit more careful about spacing them. You knit to 1 stitch before the stitch on which you've placed the button on the other band, and bind off 2 stitches. Knit to 1 stitch before the stitch on which you've placed the next button on the other band, bind off 2 stitches, and so on to the end of the buttonhole row.

Three-stitch buttonholes are a little bit more complicated, only because you need to center the button in the hole. So, just as you would do with the two-stitch buttonhole, you'll knit to 1 stitch before the stitch with the button (or to 1 stitch before the marker) and bind off 3 stitches, and continue in this manner to the end of the row.

Glossary of Techniques and Abbreviations

C3B   (3-st right-twisting cable): Slip 2 sts to cn, hold to back, k1, k2 from cn.

C3F   (3-st left-twisting cable): Slip 1 st to cn, hold to front, k2, k1 from cn.

cn   Cable needle

DPN(s)   Double pointed needle(s)

Garter stitch   When knitting back and forth: Knit every row. When knitting in the round: Knit 1 row, purl 1 row.

I-cord   Using a DPN, cast on or pick up the number of sts indicated; DO NOT TURN. *Slide sts to the opposite end of needle and knit them, pulling yarn firmly across the back of the sts; rep from * to desired length. Fasten off as indicated all sts.

k2tog   Knit 2 sts together as 1 st (right-slanting decrease).

k2tog-tbl   Knit 2 sts together through the back loops (left-slanting decrease).

k3tog   Knit 3 stitches together as 1 stitch (right-slanting double decrease).

K or k   Knit

kfb   (knit front and back increase): Knit the next st through the front loop but do not drop st from needle; knit the same st through the back loop (tbl), drop st from LH needle.

LH   Left-hand

LLI   (left lifted increase): Insert RH needle into st 1 row below next st on LH needle, lift this st and place on LH needle; knit the lifted st, then knit st on LH needle.

M1   (make 1 increase): Insert LH needle from front to back under strand of yarn between the st just worked and the next st, place strand on LH needle and knit it through the back loop (tbl).

M1P   (make 1 purl): Insert LH needle from front to back under strand of yarn between the st just worked and the next st, place strand on LH needle and purl it through the back loop.

m   marker

P or p   Purl

pm   Place a marker

PSSO   Pass slipped st over

rev St st   Reverse stockinette stitch

RLI   (right lifted increase): Insert LH needle into the st 2 rows below st just worked on RH needle, lift this st and knit it.

RH   Right-hand

RS	Right side	**Seed stitch**	(multiple of 2 sts +1 in rows) Row 1 (RS): K1, *p1, k1; repeat from * across. Row 2: Knit the purl sts and purl the knit sts as they face you. Repeat Row 2 for seed st.
sk2p	Slip 1 knitwise, k2tog, PSSO (left-slanting double decrease).		
skp	Slip 1, knit 1, PSSO.		
slip m	Slip marker		
st(s)	Stitch(es)	**Seed stitch in the round**	(multiple of 2 sts) Row 1 (RS): *K1, p1; repeat from * across. Row 2: Knit the purl sts and purl the knit sts as they face you. Repeat Row 2 for seed st.
St st	Stockinette stitch. When knitting back and forth: Knit on RS rows, purl on WS rows. When knitting in the round: Knit all rows.		

RS — Right side

sk2p — Slip 1 knitwise, k2tog, PSSO (left-slanting double decrease).

skp — Slip 1, knit 1, PSSO.

slip m — Slip marker

st(s) — Stitch(es)

St st — Stockinette stitch. When knitting back and forth: Knit on RS rows, purl on WS rows. When knitting in the round: Knit all rows.

yo — Yarn over

work even — Continue in st patterns established, with no further increases or decreases.

WS — Wrong side

2x2 ribbing — (multiple of 4 sts +2 in rows; multiple of 4 sts in rounds)
Row/Rnd 1 (RS): *K2, p2; repeat from * across/around, end k2 if working rows.
Row/Rnd 2: Knit the knit sts and purl the purl sts as they face you.
Repeat row 2 for 2x2 ribbing.

3x3 ribbing — (multiple of 6 sts +3 in rows)
Row 1 (RS): K3, *p3, k3; repeat from * across.
Row 2: Knit the knit sts and purl the purl sts as they face you.
Repeat row 2 for 3x3 ribbing.

Seed stitch — (multiple of 2 sts +1 in rows)
Row 1 (RS): K1, *p1, k1; repeat from * across.
Row 2: Knit the purl sts and purl the knit sts as they face you.
Repeat Row 2 for seed st.

Seed stitch in the round — (multiple of 2 sts)
Row 1 (RS): *K1, p1; repeat from * across.
Row 2: Knit the purl sts and purl the knit sts as they face you.
Repeat Row 2 for seed st.

Short row shaping — Work the number of sts indicated in the instructions, wrap next st and turn (w&t). Work progressively longer or shorter rows as indicated in the instructions. Work wraps together with wrapped sts as you come to them, as follows: Insert RH ndl into wrap at base of wrapped st from beneath, then bring RH ndl up and into st on LH ndl, ready to work the st; knit (or purl) wrap and st tog.

Wrap and turn (w&t) — (RS) Bring yarn forward (to the purl position), slip next st to RH needle, bring yarn to back, return slipped st (which is now wrapped) to LH needle; turn, leaving remaining sts unworked. (WS) Bring yarn back (to the knit position), slip next st to RH needle, bring yarn forward (to the purl position), return slipped st (which is now wrapped) to LH needle; turn, leaving remaining sts unworked.

1

LACE CARDIGAN

These cardigans are knit from the softest blend of hand-dyed alpaca and silk. The lace details add an airiness to the cardigans, and the shaping within the lace makes them utterly feminine.

Baby's Lace Cardigan

MATERIALS

YARN

Lorna's Laces Honor
(70% baby alpaca,
30% silk; 3.5-oz/100-g,
275-yd/251-m skein)

Pewter, 1 (1, 1, 1, 2) skein

NEEDLES

US 6 (4 mm) 24-in/60-cm or
longer circular and DPN

NOTIONS

One 2.54-cm button

Darning needle

4 stitch markers

Stitch holders

GAUGE

24 sts and 30 rows
per 4 in/10 cm

SIZES ◇ SHOWN IN SIZE: 6 months

SIZE (MONTHS)	3	6	12	18	24
TO FIT CHEST MEASUREMENT (IN)	16	17	18	19	20
TO FIT CHEST MEASUREMENT (CM)	40.5	43	45.5	48.5	51

FINISHED MEASUREMENTS

	3	6	12	18	24
CHEST CIRCUMFERENCE (IN)	18	18½	20	21½	22
CHEST CIRCUMFERENCE (CM)	45.5	47.5	51	54	56
LENGTH (IN)	7¼	7¾	8¾	9½	9¾
LENGTH (CM)	18.5	19.5	20.5	24	25

DIRECTIONS ◇

Yoke

- CO 32 (36, 42, 42, 42) sts.

- Raglan setup row: (WS): Purl, placing markers as follows: P1 (1, 1, 1, 1) for front, pm, p6 (7, 8, 8, 8) for sleeve, pm, p18 (20, 24, 24, 24) for back, pm, p6 (7, 8, 8, 8) for sleeve, pm, p1 (1, 1, 1, 1) for front.

- Row 2 (RS): Kfb, slip m, kfb, [k to 1 st before m, kfb, slip m, kfb] 3 times. 8 sts increased.

- Rows 3 and 5: Purl.

- Row 4: K1, kfb, slip m, kfb, [k to 1 st before m, kfb, slip m, kfb] 3 times, knit to end.

- Row 6: K to 1 st before m, kfb, slip m, kfb, [k to 1 st before m, kfb, slip m, kfb] 3 times, k to end.

- Row 7: Purl.

- Repeat the last 2 rows 3 (3, 3, 3, 3) times. 80 (84, 90, 90, 90) sts total; 7 (7, 7, 7, 7) sts for each front.

Front Neckline Shaping

- Row 14 (RS): Kfb, k to 1 st before m, kfb, slip m, kfb, [k to 1 st before m, kfb, slip m, kfb] 3 times, k to last st, kfb. 10 sts increased.

- Row 15 and all WS rows: Purl.

- Repeat the last 2 rows twice more. 110 (114, 120, 120, 120) sts total; 13 (13, 13, 13, 13) sts for each front, 24 (25, 26, 26, 26) sts for each sleeve, and 36 (38, 42, 42, 42) sts for back.

- Row 20 (RS): Using the "knitting on" method, CO 5 (6, 8, 8, 8) sts, k to 1 st before m, kfb, slip m, kfb, [k to 1 st before m, kfb, slip m, kfb] 3 times, knit to end.

- Row 21: Using the "purling on" method, CO 5 (6, 8, 8, 8) sts, purl to end. 19 (20, 22, 22, 22) sts for each front, 26 (27, 28, 28, 28) sts for each sleeve, and 38 (40, 44, 44, 44) sts for back.

Finish Yoke

- Row 22: [K to 1 st before m, kfb, slip m, kfb] 4 times, k to end.

- Row 23: Purl.

- Repeat these 2 rows 2 (4, 5, 6, 7) times to 22 (25, 28, 29, 30) sts in each front, 32 (37, 40, 42, 44) sts in each sleeve, and 44 (50, 56, 58, 60) sts in back. 152 (174, 192, 200, 208) total sts.

Separate Sleeves from the Body

- Knit across 22 (25, 28, 29, 30) front sts. Place next 32 (37, 40, 42, 44) sleeve sts on holder to be worked later. Using the knit-on cast-on method, CO 10 (6, 4, 6, 6) sts at underarm, placing a marker at the center of these sts to divide front from back. Knit across 44 (50, 56, 58, 60) back sts. Place next 32 (37, 40, 42, 44) sleeve sts on holder to be worked later. CO 10 (6, 4, 6, 6) sts at underarm, placing a marker to divide front from back. 108 (112, 120, 128, 132) total body sts on the needle.

- Work even in St st for 15 (15, 19, 23, 23) rows.

Begin Working Lace Rib Trim

- Row 1 (WS): Purl, increasing 0 (3, 7, 1, 5) sts evenly spaced across row. 108 (115, 127, 129, 137) total sts.

- Row 2 (RS): K7 (5, 5, 6, 5), *work Baby Lace Rib Chart (see page 26), k5, repeat from *, ending k2 (0, 0, 1, 0).

- Row 3 (WS): P7 (5, 5, 6, 5), *work chart, p5, repeat from * ending p2 (0, 0, 1, 0).

- Repeat the last 2 rows through row 12 of chart.

- BO loosely.

Sleeves

- Transfer sts from holder to DPN. Pick up and knit 10 (6, 4, 6, 6) sts CO at body underarm.

- Round 1: Knit.

- Round 2: Begin working Baby Sleeve Lace Chart (see page 26). Repeat chart 7 (7, 7, 8, 8) times around, p0 (1, 2, 0, 2).

- Continue as set through row 12 of chart.

- Purl 2 rounds. Bind off.

Button Bands

RIGHT FRONT

- With RS facing, and beginning at hem edge, pick up and knit 2 sts for every 3 rows.

- Row 1 (WS): Knit.

- Row 2 (RS): K to last 4 sts, BO 2 sts, k to end.

- Row 3: Knit, casting on 2 sts over the 2 sts bound off for buttonhole.

- Row 4: Knit.

- Bind off.

LEFT FRONT

- With RS facing, and beginning at left neckline edge, pick up and knit the same number of sts picked up for right front band.

- Knit 4 rows.

- Bind off.

Mother's Lace Cardigan

MATERIALS

YARN

Lorna's Laces Honor (70% baby alpaca, 30% silk; 3.5-oz/100-g, 275-yd/251-m skein)

Pewter, 4 (5, 5, 6, 6, 7) skeins

NEEDLES

US 4 (3.5 mm) 24-in/60-cm or longer circular and DPN

US 6 (4 mm) 24-in/60-cm or longer circular and DPN

NOTIONS

Nine ³/₄-in (2-cm) buttons

Darning needle

4 stitch markers

Stitch holders

GAUGE

24 st and 30 rows per 4 in/10 cm

SIZES ◇ SHOWN IN SIZE: 34

SIZES	XS	S	M	L	1X	2X
TO FIT ACTUAL CHEST MEASUREMENT(IN)	30	34	38	42	46	50
TO FIT ACTUAL CHEST MEASUREMENT(CM)	76	86.5	96.5	106.5	117	127

FINISHED MEASUREMENTS

	XS	S	M	L	1X	2X
FINISHED CHEST CIRCUMFERENCE(IN)	32½	36	40	44	48	52
FINISHED CHEST CIRCUMFERENCE(CM)	83	91.5	101.5	112	122	132
LENGTH (IN)	21½	22	23	23½	24	24½
LENGTH (CM)	54.5	56	58.5	59.5	61	61/62

DIRECTIONS ◇

Yoke

- CO 62 (62, 78, 78, 86, 86) sts.

- Row 1 (WS): Purl, placing markers as follows: p1 (1, 1, 1, 1, 1) for front, pm, p12 (12, 16, 16, 18, 18) for sleeve, pm, p36 (36, 44, 44, 48, 48) for back, pm, p12 (12, 16, 16, 18, 18) for sleeve, pm, p1 (1, 1, 1, 1, 1) for front.

- Row 2: Kfb, slip m, kfb, [k to 1 st before m, kfb, slip m, kfb] 3 times.

- Rows 3 and 5 (WS): Purl.

- Row 4: K1, kfb, slip m, kfb, [k to 1 st before m, kfb, slip m, kfb] 3 times, k1.

- Row 6: [K to 1 st before m, k1b, slip m, kfb] 4 times, k to end.

- Row 7: Purl.

- Repeat the last 2 rows 3 (3, 3, 3, 3, 3) times. 7 (7, 7, 7, 7, 7) sts for each front. 110 (110, 126, 126, 134, 134) sts total.

Front Neckline Shaping

- Row 14 (RS): Kfb, [k to 1 st before m, kfb, slip m, kfb] 4 times, knit to last st, kfb. 10 sts increased.

- Row 15: Purl.

- Repeat these 2 rows 5 more times. 19 (19, 19, 19, 19, 19) sts in each front, 36 (36, 40, 40, 42, 42), sts in each sleeve, and 60 (60, 68, 68, 72, 72) sts in back.

- Row 26 (RS): Using the "knitting on" method, CO 11 (11, 15, 15, 17, 17) sts, (k to 1 st before m, kfb, slip m, kfb) 4 times, k to end.

- Row 27: Using the "purling on" method, CO 11 (11, 15, 15, 17, 17) sts, purl to end. 31 (31, 35, 35, 37, 37) sts in each front, 38 (38, 42, 42, 44, 44) sts in each sleeve, and 62 (62, 70, 70, 74, 74) sts in back.

Finish Yoke

- Row 28: [K to 1 st before m, kfb, slip m, kfb] 4 times, k to end.

- Row 29: Purl.

- Repeat these 2 rows 13 (15, 16, 18, 18, 19) times more.

Separate Sleeves from the Body

- Next row (RS): K across front 45 (47, 52, 54, 56, 57) sts, place next 66 (70, 76, 80, 82, 84) sts on holder to be worked later, CO 8 (14, 16, 24, 32, 42) sts at underarm, knit across back 90 (94, 104, 108, 112, 114) sts, place next 66 (70, 76, 80, 82, 84) sts on holder to be worked later, CO 8 (14, 16, 24, 32, 42) sts at underarm, knit across front 45 (47, 52, 54, 56, 57) sts. 196 (216, 240, 264, 288, 312) total body sts.

Body

- Row 1 (WS): Purl.

- Row 2 (RS): Knit, increasing 0 (3, 3, 3, 3, 3)/ decreasing 1 (0, 0, 0, 0, 0) sts evenly across for a multiple of 6, plus 3. 195 (219, 243, 267, 291, 315) total sts.

- Work in St st for 3 (3, 3½, 3½, 4, 4) in/7.5 (7.5, 9, 9, 10, 10) cm, ending with a WS row.

Begin Rib Patterning

- Row 1 (RS): K4, p1 (k5, p1) to last 4 sts, k4.

- Row 2 (WS): P4 (k1, p5) to last 5 sts, k1, p4.

- Repeat these 2 rows 14 more times.

Begin Waistline Ribbing

- Change to smaller needle.

- Row 1 (RS): (K3, p3) to last 3 sts, k3.

- Row 2 (WS): (P3, k3) to last 3 sts, p3.

- Repeat these 2 rows 10 more times. The sweater measures approximately 9½ (9½, 10, 10, 10½, 10½) in/24 (24, 25.5, 25.5, 26.5, 26.5) cm from the underarm.

- Change back to larger needle.

Begin Working Mother Lace Chart 1
(see also Mother Lace Chart 1 on page 27)

- Row 1 (RS): K3, repeat lace chart 1 to last 6 sts, p3, k3.

- Row 2 (WS): P3, k3, repeat lace chart 1 to last 3 sts, p3.

- Continue as established, working through all 12 rows of lace chart 1 twice (24 rows total).

Begin Working Mother Lace Chart 2
(see also Mother Lace Chart 2 on page 27)

- Row 1 (RS): K3, repeat lace chart 2 to last 6 sts, p3, m1P, k3.

- Row 2 (WS): P3, k4, repeat lace chart 2 to last 3 sts, p3.

- Continue as established, working through all 12 rows of lace chart 2 once (12 rows total).

- BO loosely.

Sleeves

- Transfer 66 (70, 76, 80, 82, 84) sleeve sts from holder to DPN.

- Round 1: Knit across 66 (70, 76, 80, 82, 84) sleeve sts, pick up and knit 8 (14, 16, 24, 32, 42) sts CO at body underarm. 74 (84, 92, 104, 114, 126) sleeve sts.

- Work in St st for 23 (23, 26, 26, 30, 30) more rows.

- Next round, decrease 2 (0, 2, 2, 0, 0) sts evenly.

Begin Stitch Patterning

- Round 1: (K5, p1) around.

- Repeat this round 29 more times.

Begin Ribbing

- Change to smaller needle.

- Round 1: (K3, p3) around.

- Repeat this round 35 (41, 41, 43, 40, 40) more times.

- Change back to larger needle.

Begin Lace Charts

- Work through the 12 rows of lace chart 1 twice (24 rows total), then work through the 12 rows of lace chart 2 once.

- BO loosely.

Button Bands

RIGHT FRONT

- Using smaller needle and with RS facing, and beginning at hem edge, pick up and knit 2 sts for every 3 rows.

- Row 1 (WS): Knit.

- Row 2 (RS): Knit, making a buttonhole every 2 in/5 cm by binding off 2 sts.

- Row 3: Knit, casting on 2 sts over the bound-off sts to complete buttonholes.

- Row 4: Knit.

- Bind off.

LEFT FRONT

- Using smaller needle and with RS facing, and beginning at left neckline edge, pick up and knit the same number of sts picked up for right front band.

- Work 4 rows in garter stitch.

- Bind off.

Finishing

- Weave in ends.

- Block.

- Attach buttons.

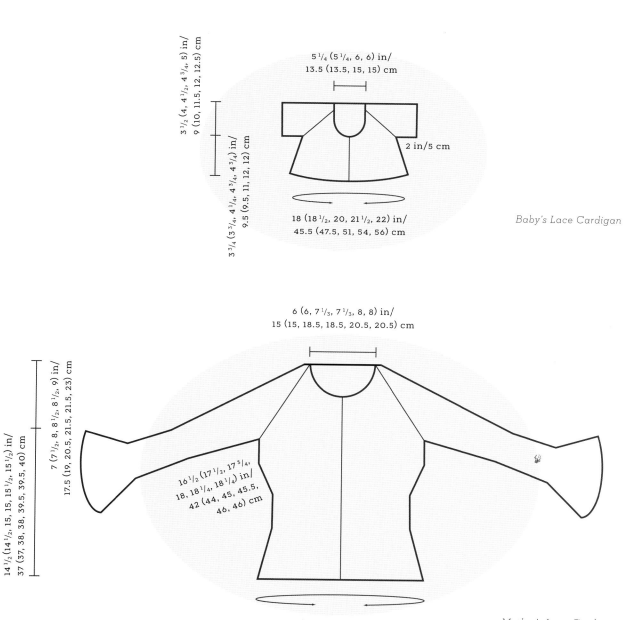

5 1/4 (5 1/4, 6, 6) in/
13.5 (13.5, 15, 15) cm

3 1/2 (4, 4 1/2, 4 3/4, 5) in/
9 (10, 11.5, 12, 12.5) cm

3 3/4 (3 3/4, 4 1/4, 4 3/4, 4 3/4) in/
9.5 (9.5, 11, 12, 12) cm

2 in/5 cm

18 (18 1/2, 20, 21 1/2, 22) in/
45.5 (47.5, 51, 54, 56) cm

Baby's Lace Cardigan

6 (6, 7 1/3, 7 1/3, 8, 8) in/
15 (15, 18.5, 18.5, 20.5, 20.5) cm

7 (7 1/2, 8, 8 1/2, 8 1/2, 9) in/
17.5 (19, 20.5, 21.5, 21.5, 23) cm

14 1/2 (14 1/2, 15, 15, 15 1/2, 15 1/2) in/
37 (37, 38, 38, 39.5, 39.5, 40) cm

16 1/2 (17 1/2, 17 3/4,
18, 18 1/4, 18 1/4) in/
42 (44, 45, 45.5,
46, 46) cm

32 1/2 (36, 40, 44, 48, 52) in/
83 (91.5, 101.5, 112, 122, 132) cm

Mother's Lace Cardigan

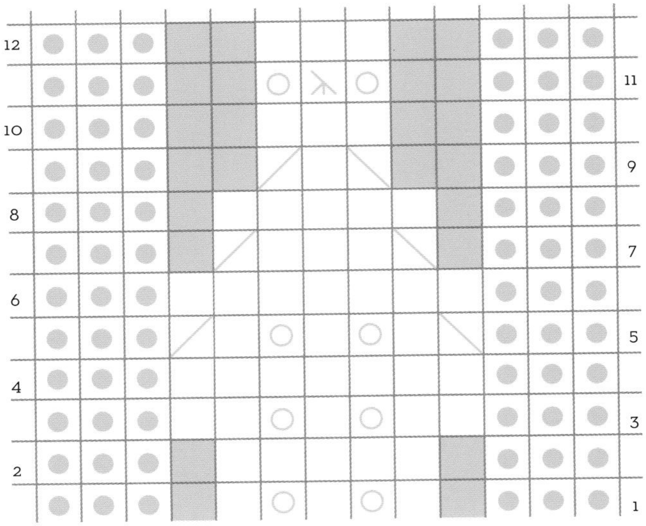

Legend (left chart):

	KNIT ON RS, PURL ON WS		SSK
	PURL ON RS, KNIT ON WS		K2TOG
	NO STITCH		SL1 K2TOG PSSO
	YO		

Legend (right chart):

	KNIT ON RS, PURL ON WS		SSK
	PURL ON RS, KNIT ON WS		K2TOG
	NO STITCH		SL1 K2TOG PSSO
	YO		

Baby Lace Rib Chart

- R1 (RS): p3, k1, yo, k1, yo, k1, p3
- R2 (WS): k3, p5, k3
- R3: p3, k2, yo, k1, yo, k2, p3
- R4: k3, p7, k3
- R5: p3, ssk, k1, yo, k1, yo, k1, k2tog, p3
- R6: K3, p7, k3
- R7: p3, ssk, k3, k2tog, p3
- R8: k3, p5, k3
- R9: p3, ssk, k1, k2tog, p3
- R10: k3, p3, k3
- R11: p3, yo, sl1 k2tog psso, yo, p3
- R12: k3, p3, k3

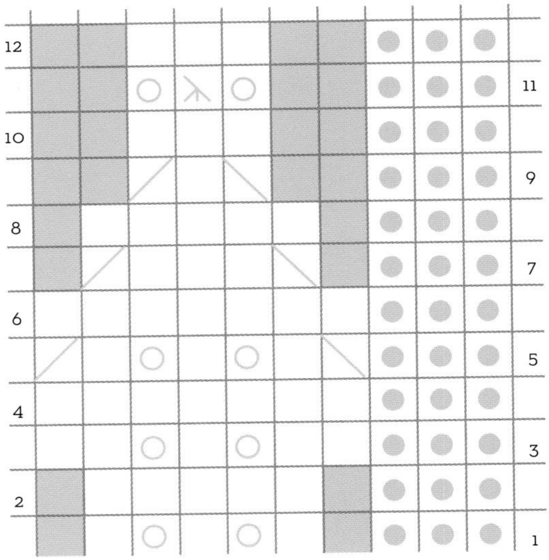

Baby Sleeve Lace Chart

- R1 (RS): p3, k1, yo, k1, yo, k1
- R2 (WS): p5, k3
- R3: p3, k2, yo, k1, yo, k2,
- R4: p7, k3
- R5: p3, ssk, k1, yo, k1, yo, k1, k2tog
- R6: p7, k3
- R7: p3, ssk, k3, k2tog
- R8: p5, k3
- R9: p3, ssk, k1, k2tog
- R10: p3, k3
- R11: p3, yo, sl1 k2tog psso, yo
- R12: p3, k3

Legend (Chart 1):

- ☐ KNIT ON RS, PURL ON WS
- ⊙ PURL ON RS, KNIT ON WS
- ▨ NO STITCH
- ◯ YO
- ◺ SSK
- ◿ K2TOG
- 𝛌 SL1 K2TOG PSSO

Legend (Chart 2):

- ☐ KNIT ON RS, PURL ON WS
- ⊙ PURL ON RS, KNIT ON WS
- ▨ NO STITCH
- ◯ YO
- ◺ SSK
- ◿ K2TOG
- 𝛌 SL1 K2TOG PSSO
- M MAKE ONE

Mother Lace Chart 1

- R1 (RS): p3, k1, yo, k1, yo, k1
- R2 (WS): p5, k3
- R3: p3, k2, yo, k1, yo, k2,
- R4: p7, k3
- R5: p3, ssk, k1, yo, k1, yo, k1, k2tog
- R6: p7, k3
- R7: p3, ssk, k3, k2tog
- R8: p5, k3
- R9: p3, ssk, k1, k2tog
- R10: p3, k3
- R11: p3, yo, sl1 k2tog psso, yo
- R12: p3, k3

Mother Lace Chart 2

- R1 (RS): p3, m1, k1, yo, k1, yo, k1
- R2 (WS): p5, k4
- R3: p4, k2, yo, k1, yo, k2,
- R4: p7, k3
- R5: p4, ssk, k1, yo, k1, yo, k1, k2tog
- R6: p7, k4
- R7: p4, ssk, k3, k2tog
- R8: p5, k4
- R9: p4, ssk, k1, k2tog
- R10: p3, k4
- R11: p4, yo, sl1 k2tog psso, yo
- R12: p3, k4

2

SURFER TEE

This casual tee is knit from a luxurious camel, merino, and silk blend that is soft and warm at the same time. The optional front kangaroo pocket is perfect for carrying pebbles and beach glass or tissues and snacks during a seaside outing.

The child's version has short sleeves, which can be lengthened by simply working the sleeve even in stockinette stitch to your desired length and then adding the seed stitch border. The fronts of the sweaters are also adorned by twisted lace stitch columns that are easy-to-work yet visually striking twisted lace.

Child's Surfer Tee

MATERIALS

YARN
*Conjoined Creations Icon
(15% camel, 15% silk,
70% merino; 1.75-oz/50-g,
98-yd/90-m skein)*

*Vidal Sassoon
5 (6, 7, 8, 9) skeins*

NEEDLES
*Size 7 (4.5 mm)
24-in/60-cm circular and
DPN, or size needed to
match gauge*

*Size 5 (3.75 mm)
24-in/60-cm circular and
DPN*

NOTIONS
Darning needle

6 stitch markers

*2 stitch holders or lengths
of waste yarn*

GAUGE
*18 sts and 24 rows per
4 in/10 cm in stockinette
stitch*

SIZES ◇ SHOWN IN SIZE: 8

SIZES	4	6	8	10
TO FIT (IN)	23	25	27	28
TO FIT (CM)	58.5	63.5	68.5	71

FINISHED MEASUREMENTS

	4	6	8	10
CHEST CIRCUMFERENCE (IN)	25¾	27½	29¼	31
CHEST CIRCUMFERENCE (CM)	65.5	70	74.5	79
LENGTH (IN)	15	16½	18	19¾
LENGTH (CM)	38	42	45.5	50

DIRECTIONS ◇

NOTE: The top is worked back and forth in rows to create the yoke opening, then joined for working in the round. Raglan shaping is worked each side of markers.

Yoke

- CO 60 (60, 72, 72) sts.

- Establish edge sts and place markers (pm) for raglan shaping as follows:

- Setup row (WS): K5 (edge sts—maintain in garter stitch), p6 (6, 8, 8) for front, pm, p8 (8, 10, 10) for sleeve, pm, p22 (22, 26, 26) for back, pm, p8 (8, 10, 10) for sleeve, pm, p6 (6, 8, 8), k5 (edge sts) for front.

- Row 1 (RS): K5 (edge sts) k3, [yo, sk2p, yo] for lace column, *knit to 1 st before m, kfb, slip m, kfb; repeat from * 3 times, knit to last 11 sts, [yo, sk2p, yo], knit to end—8 sts increased; 1 on each front, 2 each on sleeves and back.

- Row 2: K5, purl to last 5 sts, K5.

- Maintaining garter stitch edging and lace columns on each front, and remaining sts in St st, repeat last 2 rows 17 (19, 19, 21) times, ending with a WS row—29 (31, 33, 35) sts each front, 58 (62, 66, 70) sts for back, and 44 (48, 50, 54) sts each sleeve; 204 (220, 232, 248) sts.

Separate Sleeves and Join the Body

- Next row (RS): Removing extra markers as you come to them, pm at center of each underarm between back and fronts and at center front for beginning of round as follows: k29 (31, 33, 35) front sts; place next 44 (48, 50, 54) sleeve sts on holder, pm, k58 (62, 66, 70) back sts, pm, place next 44 (48, 50, 54) sleeve sts on holder, k29 (31, 33, 35) front sts, pm (center front)—116 (124, 132, 140) body sts. Join to work in the round.

Body

- Discontinue garter stitch edging at center front and work center front sts in St st for remainder of piece. Continue lace columns every other round as set, knitting these sts on alternate rounds, and work remaining sts in St st.

- Work even for 48 (54, 60, 66) rounds—piece measures approximately 8 (9, 10, 11) in/20.5 (23, 25.5, 28) cm from underarm.

Lower Border

- Knit around to just under armhole, k2tog.

- Change to smaller needle and work in seed st for 6 (6, 10, 10) rounds.

- BO all sts in pattern.

Sleeves

(work both the same)

- Transfer 44 (48, 50, 54) sleeve sts from holder to circular needle or DPN. Join for working in the round; pm at underarm center for beginning of round. Change to smaller needle, k2tog and work in seed st for 6 (6, 10, 10) rounds.

- BO all sts in pattern.

Pocket

- CO 28 (28, 32, 32) sts.

- Row 1 (WS): K5 for garter stitch edging, purl across to last 5 sts, k5 for garter stitch edging.

- Row 2: Knit.

- Repeat last 2 rows 5 (5, 9, 9) more times, then work row 1 once more.

- Next row—increase row (RS): K5, RLI, knit across to last 5 sts, LLI, k5—2 sts increased.

- Next row (WS): K5, purl to last 5 sts, k5.

- Repeat the last 2 rows 4 more times, 38 (38, 42, 42) sts.

- Work 6 (6, 10, 10) rows even, keeping edge sts in garter stitch, and remaining sts in St st. Bind off.

Finishing

- Seam underarm closed, if necessary.

- Attach pocket, taking care to center it.

- Weave in ends.

Mother's Surfer Tee

MATERIALS

YARN
Conjoined Creations Icon
(15% camel, 15% silk,
70% merino; 1.75-oz/50-g,
98-yd/90-m skein)

Jacques Cousteau,
9 (9, 10, 11, 12, 13) skeins

NEEDLES
Size 7 (4.5 mm)
24-in/60-cm circular and
DPN, or size needed to
match gauge

Size 5 (3.75 mm)
24-in/60-cm circular and
DPN

NOTIONS
Darning needle

6 stitch markers

2 stitch holders or lengths
of waste yarn

GAUGE
18 sts and 24 rows per
4 in/10 cm in stockinette
stitch

SIZES ◇ SHOWN IN SIZE: 34

SIZES	XS	S	M	L	1X	2X
TO FIT BUST (IN)	30	34	38	42	46	50
TO FIT BUST (CM)	76	86.5	96.5	106.5	117	127

FINISHED MEASUREMENTS

BUST (IN)	32½	36	40	44	48	52
BUST (CM)	82.5	91.5	101.5	112	122	132
LENGTH (IN)	23¼	24 ½	25 ½	26¼	27	27½
LENGTH (CM)	59	62	65	66.5	68.5	70

DIRECTIONS ◇

NOTE: The sweater is worked back and forth in rows to create the yoke open-ing and then joined for working in the round. Raglan shaping is worked on each side of markers.

Yoke

- CO 80 (80, 86, 86, 98, 98) sts.

- Establish edge sts and place markers (pm) for raglan shaping as follows:

- Setup row (WS): K5 to form garter stitch edging, p10 (10, 11, 11, 13, 13) for front, pm, p10 (10, 11, 11, 13, 13) for sleeve, pm, p30 (30, 32, 32, 36, 36) for back, pm, p10 (10, 11, 11, 13, 13) for sleeve, pm, p10 (10, 11, 11, 13, 13), k5 (garter edging) for front.

- Row 1 (RS): K5 edge sts, k5, [yo, sk2p, yo] for lace column, *knit to 1 st before m, kfb, slip m, kfb; repeat from * 3 times, knit to last 13 sts, [yo, sk2p, yo], knit to end—8 sts increased; 1 for each front, 2 for each sleeve and back.

- Row 2: K5, purl to last 5 sts, K5.

- Repeat the last 2 rows 20 (22, 23, 25, 25, 26) times, maintaining garter edging and lace columns, ending with a WS row. 248 (264, 278, 294, 306, 314) sts; 36 (38, 40, 42, 44, 45) sts each front, 72 (76, 80, 84, 88, 90) sts for back, and 52 (56, 59, 63, 65, 67) sts each sleeve.

Separate Sleeves and Join the Body

- Next row (RS): Remove extra markers as you come to them, and pm at center of each under-arm and at center front for beginning of round as follows: K36 (38, 40, 42, 44, 45) front sts, place next 52 (56, 59, 63, 65, 67) sleeve sts on holder, using the backward loop method, CO 1 (5, 10, 15, 20, 27) sts for underarm, k72 (76, 80, 84, 88, 90) back sts, place next 52 (56, 59, 63, 65, 67) sleeve sts on holder, CO 1 (5, 10, 15, 20, 27) sts for underarm, k36 (38, 40, 42, 44, 45) front sts, pm (center front)—146 (162, 180, 198, 216, 234) sts for body. Join to work in the round.

Body

- Discontinue garter stitch edging at center front and work these sts in St st for remainder of piece. Maintain lace columns as set every other round and knit these sts on alternate rounds; work the remaining sts in St st.

- Work even for 78 (81, 84, 84, 87, 90) rounds, or 2.5 in/6 cm short of total desired length; piece measures 13 (13½, 14, 14, 14½, 15) in/33 (34, 35.5, 35.5, 37, 38) cm from underarm.

Lower Border

- Knit around to just under armhole.

- Change to smaller needles, k2tog, and work in seed st for 14 rounds.

- BO all sts in pattern.

Sleeve

- Transfer 52 (56, 59, 63, 65, 67) sleeve sts from holder to circular needle or DPN. Pick up and knit 1 (5, 10, 15, 20, 27) sts in sts CO at under-arm—53 (61, 69, 78, 85, 94) sts. Join for work-ing in the round; pm at center of underarm for beginning of round. Work in St st for 86 (93, 96, 98, 98, 98) rounds—14¼ (15½, 16, 16¼, 16¼, 16¼) in/36 (39.5, 40.5, 41, 41, 41) cm.

Cuff

- Change to smaller needle and work in seed st for 14 rounds.

- BO all sts in pattern.

Pocket (Optional)

- Maintain first and last 5 sts in garter stitch throughout.

- CO 36 sts.

- Row 1 (WS): K5 for garter stitch edging, purl across to last 5 sts, k5 for edging.

- Row 2: Knit.

- Repeat last 2 rows 12 more times.

- Repeat row 1 once more.

- Next row—increase row (RS): K5, RLI, knit across to last 5 sts, LLI, k5—2 sts increased.

- Next row (WS): K5, purl to last 5 sts, k5.

- Repeat last 2 rows 4 more times, 46 sts.

- Work 15 rows even, keeping edge sts in garter stitch. Bind off.

Neckline Trim:

- With smaller needle, RS facing and beginning at right front neck, pick up and knit 1 st for every st cast on around neckline.

- Row 1 (WS): Knit.

- Row 2: Knit.

- Bind off loosely.

Finishing

- Weave in ends.

- Seam underarm closed, if necessary.

- Attach pocket, taking care to center it.

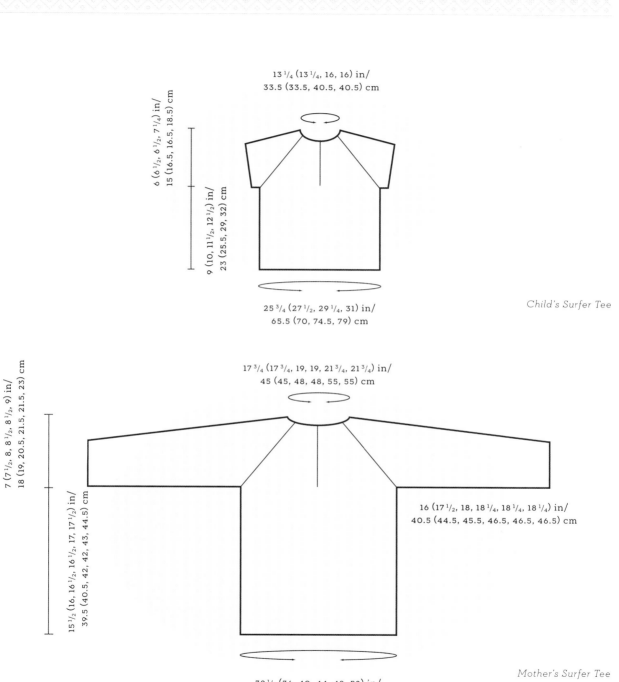

13 1/4 (13 1/4, 16, 16) in/
33.5 (33.5, 40.5, 40.5) cm

6 (6 1/2, 6 1/2, 7 1/4) in/
15 (16.5, 16.5, 18.5) cm

9 (10, 11 1/2, 12 1/2) in/
23 (25.5, 29, 32) cm

25 3/4 (27 1/2, 29 1/4, 31) in/
65.5 (70, 74.5, 79) cm

Child's Surfer Tee

17 3/4 (17 3/4, 19, 19, 21 3/4, 21 3/4) in/
45 (45, 48, 48, 55, 55) cm

7 (7 1/2, 8, 8 1/2, 8 1/2, 9) in/
18 (19, 20.5, 21.5, 21.5, 23) cm

15 1/2 (16, 16 1/2, 16 1/2, 17, 17 1/2) in/
39.5 (40.5, 42, 42, 43, 44.5) cm

16 (17 1/2, 18, 18 1/4, 18 1/4, 18 1/4) in/
40.5 (44.5, 45.5, 46.5, 46.5, 46.5) cm

32 1/2 (36, 40, 44, 48, 52) in/
82.5 (91.5, 101.5, 112, 122, 132) cm

Mother's Surfer Tee

3

ARAN COAT

These sweaters are a play on the classic Aran style. The cables themselves are very traditional, but the shape of the sweaters gives them a modern look. You'll create the peplum on the baby's sweater and the hip shaping on the mother's version simply by increasing the number of stitches between the cables. Knit in a chunky wash-and-wear yarn, these sweaters are quick to make and easy to care for.

Baby's Aran Coat

MATERIALS

YARN

Berroco Vintage Chunky (50% acrylic, 40% wool, 10% nylon; 3.5-oz/100-g, 220-yd/202-m skein)

Color 6175, 2 (2, 2, 3, 3) skeins

NEEDLES

Size 9 (5.5 mm) 24-in/60-cm circular and DPN, or size needed to match gauge

Size 7 (4.5 mm) 24-in/60-cm circular

NOTIONS

Four ³⁄₄-in/19-mm buttons

Darning needle

4 stitch markers of one color for raglan seams

12 stitch markers of a contrasting color for cables

2 stitch holders or lengths of waste yarn

GAUGE

14 sts and 24 rows per 4 in/10 cm in garter stitch, using larger needle

SIZES ◇ SHOWN IN SIZE: 6 MONTHS

SIZE (MONTHS)	3	6	12	18	24
TO FIT CHEST (IN)	16	17	18	19	20
TO FIT CHEST (CM)	40.5	43	45.5	48.5	51

FINISHED MEASUREMENTS

	3	6	12	18	24
CHEST CIRCUMFERENCE (IN)	18	19½	22	23	24
CHEST CIRCUMFERENCE (CM)	45.5	49.5	56	58.5	61
LENGTH (IN)	10	10¾	12¾	14¾	17½
LENGTH (CM)	25.5	27	32	37.5	44

DIRECTIONS ◇

Yoke

- The sweater is worked in garter stitch; you will work cable 1 once along the edges of the two fronts, centered on each sleeve, and twice down the center of the back.

- Using larger circular needle, CO 28 (32, 40, 40, 40) sts, placing 4 markers (pm) as follows for raglan shaping: CO 5 (6, 7, 7, 7) sts for front, pm, CO 4 (4, 6, 6, 6) sts for sleeve, pm, CO 10 (12, 14, 14, 14) sts for back, pm, CO 4 (4, 6, 6, 6) sts for sleeve, pm, CO 5 (6, 7, 7, 7) sts for front.

- Rows 1, 3 and 5 (RS): [Knit to 1 st before m, kfb, slip m, kfb] 4 times, knit to end—8 sts increased each row; 1 on each front, 2 on each sleeve and back—52 (56, 64, 64, 64) sts after row 5; 8 (9, 10, 10, 10) sts each front, 10 (10, 12, 12, 12) sts each sleeve, 16 (18, 20, 20, 20) sts for back.

- Rows 2 and 4: Knit.

Establish cables

- Using contrasting color markers and beginning with row 2 of cable 1 (*see Baby's Cable Chart 1 on page 48*), work as follows:

- Row 6 (WS): K2, place cable marker (pcm), work cable across next 6 sts, pcm, k0 (1, 2, 2, 2), slip m; k2 (2, 3, 3, 3), pcm, work cable, pcm, k2 (2, 3, 3, 3) slip m; k1 (2, 3, 3, 3), pcm, work cable, pcm, k2, pcm, work cable, pcm, k1 (2, 3, 3, 3), slip m; k2 (2, 3, 3, 3), pcm, work cable, pcm, k2 (2, 3, 3, 3) slip m; k0 (1, 2, 2, 2), pcm, work cable, pcm, k2.

- Row 7 (RS): Working the next row of cable 1 between cable markers as you encounter them, and knitting remaining sts, *work to 1 st before raglan m, kfb, sl m, kfb, rep from * 3 more times, work to the end of row—8 sts increased; 60 (64, 72, 72, 72) sts.

- Row 8 (WS): Work even in garter stitch, working next row of cable 1 as established between each set of cable markers.

- Repeat last 2 rows 7 (7, 8, 9, 10) more times— 16 (17, 19, 20, 21) sts each front, 26 (26, 30, 32, 34) sts each sleeve, and 32 (34, 38, 40, 42) sts for back; 116 (120, 136, 144, 152) sts total.

Separate Sleeves from the Body

- Next row (RS): Continuing in pattern as established, work 16 (17, 19, 20, 21) front sts, place 26 (26, 30, 32, 34) sleeve sts on a holder, work 32 (34, 38, 40, 42) back sts, place 26 (26, 30, 32, 34) sleeve sts on a holder, work remaining 16 (17, 19, 20, 21) front sts—64 (68, 76, 80, 84) sts for body. Make note of last round of cable worked for sleeves.

Body

- Work through row 4 of the cable, then work the 4 rows of the cable 0 (0, 1, 1, 2) times more.

Create Additional Cables

- Next row (row 1 of cable 1) (RS): K2, work cable 1 across next 6 sts as established, k2, work cable 1, k to 8 st before back cable, work cable 1, k2, work cable 1, k2, work cable 1, k2, work cable 1, knit to 8 sts before front cable, work cable, k2, work cable, k2—4 cables added; 8 cables total.

- Work 3 (7, 11, 11, 15) rows even in patts established, ending with row 4 of cable 1.

Switch to Cable 2

- You will now work cable 2 instead of cable 1 for each of the 8 cables. (*See Baby's Cable Chart 2 on page 48.*)

- Next row: K2, work row 1 of cable 2, k2, work cable 2, k to next cable, work cable 2, k2, work cable 2, k2, work cable 2, k2, work cable 2, k to next cable, work cable 2, k2, work cable 2, k2.

- Working patterns as established, work rows 2–14 once, then work rows 11–14 (shown in the boxed area of chart) 2 (2, 3, 5, 7) times.

- Bind off.

Sleeves

- Transfer 26 (26, 30, 32, 34) sts to circular or DPN needles. Join; pm for beginning of round.

- Continuing in pattern established (cable 1 and garter stitch), work even until sleeve measures 6 (6½, 7½, 8, 8½) in/15.5 (16.5, 19, 20.5, 21.5) cm from underarm. Discontinue cable.

Cuff

- Bind off.

Button Band

BUTTONHOLE BAND

- With RS facing and larger needle, begin at lower right front edge, pick up and knit 1 st for every 2 rows up front to neck edge.

BUTTONHOLES

- Row 1 (WS): K2, [BO 2 sts for buttonhole, k3] 4 times, knit to end.

- Row 2: Knit and CO 2 sts over each 2 bound-off sts from previous row.

- BO all sts loosely.

BUTTON BAND

- With RS facing and larger needle, begin at left front neck edge, pick up and knit 1 st for every 2 rows down front to lower edge. Knit 2 rows.

- BO all sts loosely.

Finishing

- Weave in ends, attach buttons, seam underarm, if necessary.

- Block to desired length.

NOTE: Garter stitch responds well to blocking. If your row tension is tight, you may need to lightly steam your sweater while stretching or pinning it to the desired length.

Mother's Aran Coat

MATERIALS

YARN

Berroco Vintage Chunky (50% acrylic, 40% wool, 10% nylon; 3.5-oz/100-g, 220-yd/202-m skein)

Color: 6175, 6 (7, 7, 8, 9, 9) skeins

NEEDLES

Size 9 (5.5 mm) 24-in/60-cm circular and DPN, or size needed to match gauge

Size 7 (4.5 mm) 24-in/60-cm circular

NOTIONS

Six ³/₄-in/19-mm buttons

Darning needle

4 stitch markers of one color for raglan seams

12 stitch markers of a contrasting color for cables

2 stitch holders or lengths of waste yarn

GAUGE

14 sts and 24 rows per 4 in/10 cm in garter stitch, using larger needle

SIZES ◇ SHOWN IN SIZE: 36

SIZES	XS	S	M	L	1X	2X	3X
TO FIT BUST (IN)	28	32	36	40	44	48	52
TO FIT BUST (CM)	71	81.5	91.5	101.5	112	122	132

FINISHED MEASUREMENTS

	XS	S	M	L	1X	2X	3X
BUST (IN)	28½	32	36½	40	44½	48	53
BUST (CM)	72.5	81.5	93	101.5	113	122	133.5
LENGTH (IN)	17½	19	19½	21	23	24	24½
LENGTH (CM)	45	48.5	50	53.5	58.5	60	62

DIRECTIONS ◇

Collar

- Using larger circular needle, CO 46 (46, 58, 58, 58, 70, 70) sts.
- Rows 1–5: Knit (garter stitch).
- Raglan setup row (WS): K8 (8, 10, 10, 10, 12, 12) for front, pm, k7 (7, 9, 9, 9, 11, 11) for sleeve, pm, k16 (16, 20, 20, 20, 24, 24) for back, k7 (7, 9, 9, 9, 11, 11) for sleeve, k8 (8, 10, 10, 10, 12, 12) for front.

Yoke

- Row 1: Increase row (RS): [Knit to 1 st before m, kfb, slip m, kfb] 4 times, knit to end—8 sts increased; 1 on each front, 2 on each sleeve and back.

Establish Cables

- Using contrasting color markers and beginning with row 2 of Cable 1 (see *Mother's Cable Chart 1 on page 49*), work as follows:

- Row 2 (WS): K2, place cable marker (pcm), work cable 1 across next 7 sts, pcm, k0 (0, 2, 2, 2, 4, 4); slip m, k1 (1, 2, 2, 2, 3, 3), pcm, work cable 1, pcm, k1 (1, 2, 2, 2, 3, 3); slip m, k0 (0, 2, 2, 2, 4, 4), pm, work cable 1, pcm, k4, pcm, work cable 1, pcm, k0 (0, 2, 2, 2, 4, 4); slip m, k1 (1, 2, 2, 2, 3, 3), pcm, work cable 1, pcm, k1 (1, 2, 2, 2, 3, 3); slip m, k0 (0, 2, 2, 2, 4, 4), pcm, work cable 1, pcm, k2.

SIZES 28 AND 32 ONLY

- Next row (RS): Working next row of cable 1 as established between cable markers and remaining sts in garter stitch, work to first raglan m, M1; [slip m, kfb, work in pattern to 1 st before next raglan m, kfb] 3 times; slip m, M1, work in pattern to end—8 sts increased; 1 on each front, 2 on each sleeve and back.

- Next row: Work even, working cables between cable markers.

ALL OTHER SIZES

- Row 3—increase row (RS): Working next row of cable 1 as established between cable markers and remaining sts in garter stitch [work to 1 st before raglan m, kfb, slip m, kfb] 4 times, work to end—8 sts increased; 1 on each front, 2 on each sleeve and back.

- Row 4 (WS): Work even slipping markers, working next row of cable 1 as established between cable markers and remaining sts in garter stitch—62 (62, 74, 74, 74, 86, 86) sts.

- Repeat rows 3 & 4 14 (17, 20, 23, 27, 25, 22) times—182 (206, 234, 258, 290, 286, 262) sts; 25 (28, 32, 35, 39, 39, 36) each front, 50 (56, 64, 70, 78, 78, 72) for back, and 41 (47, 53, 59, 67, 65, 59) each sleeve.

FOR SIZES 48 AND 52 ONLY

- Work 3 (10) more rows, maintaining cable pattern and increasing at raglan markers every row, working kfb before and after markers on RS and WS rows—310 (342) sts; 42 (46) each front, 84 (92) for back, 71 (79) each sleeve. Size 48 only: Work 1 more WS row without increasing. Piece measures approximately 6 (7, 8, 9 , 10, 10, 10) in/ 15 (18, 19.5, 22, 25.5, 25.5, 25.5) cm.

Separate Sleeves and Join Body (All Sizes)

- Continuing pattern as established (cables and garter stitch), work 25 (28, 32, 35, 39, 42, 46) front sts; place 41 (47, 53, 59, 67, 71, 79) sleeve sts on a holder; work 50 (56, 64, 70, 78, 84, 92) back sts, place 41 (47, 53, 59, 67, 71, 79) sleeve sts on a holder; work remaining 25 (28, 32, 35, 39, 42, 46) front sts—100 (112, 128, 140, 156, 168, 184) sts for body.

Body

- Working even, work through row 4 of cable 1, then work the 4 rows of the cable pattern 1 (2, 2, 2, 2, 2) more times.

Begin Working Additional Cables

- K2, work cable 1 across 7 sts, k4, work cable 1, knit to 11 st before back cable, [work cable 1, k4] 3 times, work cable 1, knit to 11 sts before front cable, work cable 1, k4, work cable 1, k2. There are now 2 cables established on each front, and 4 on the back.

- Maintaining the remaining sts in garter stitch, work the 4 rows of cable 1 in each cable location a total of 4 (4, 4, 4, 4, 5, 5) times.

- Switch to cable 2 (see *Mother's Cable Chart 2 on page 49*) at each cable and work rows 1–16 one time, then work rows 13–16 only 5 (5, 5, 5, 6, 6, 7) times.

- Work 10 rows in garter stitch.

- Bind off.

Sleeves

- Transfer 41 (47, 53, 59, 67, 71, 79) sts to circular or DPN needles. Join; pm for beginning of round. Work 5 rounds in garter stitch.

- Bind off.

Button Bands

RIGHT BUTTONHOLE BAND

- With RS facing and larger needle, begin at lower right front edge, pick up and knit 1 st for every 2 rows up front to neck edge.

BUTTONHOLES

- Row 1 (WS): K2, [BO 2 for buttonhole, k3] 6 times, knit to end.

- Row 2: Knit, casting on 2 sts over each 2 bound-off sts from previous row.

- BO all sts loosely.

LEFT BUTTON BAND

- With RS facing and larger needle, begin at left front neck edge, pick up and knit 1 st for every 2 rows down front to lower edge. Knit 2 rows.

- Bind off all sts loosely.

Finishing

- Weave in ends, attach buttons, seam underarm, if necessary.

- Block to desired length.

NOTE: Garter stitch is very "blockable." If your row tension is tight, you may need to lightly steam your sweater while stretching or pinning it to the desired length.

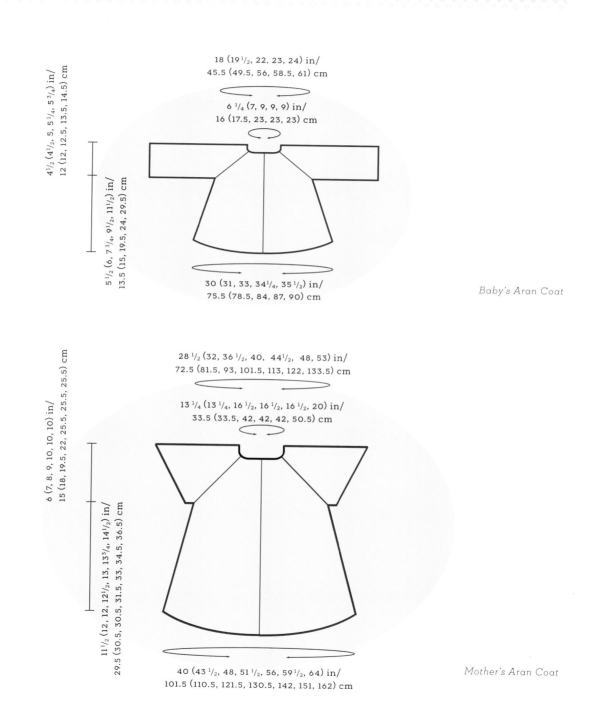

18 (19 1/2, 22, 23, 24) in/
45.5 (49.5, 56, 58.5, 61) cm

6 1/4 (7, 9, 9, 9) in/
16 (17.5, 23, 23, 23) cm

4 1/2 (4 1/2, 5, 5 1/4, 5 3/4) in/
12 (12, 12.5, 13.5, 14.5) cm

5 1/2 (6, 7 3/4, 9 1/2, 11 1/2) in/
13.5 (15, 19.5, 24, 29.5) cm

30 (31, 33, 34 1/4, 35 1/2) in/
75.5 (78.5, 84, 87, 90) cm

Baby's Aran Coat

28 1/2 (32, 36 1/2, 40, 44 1/2, 48, 53) in/
72.5 (81.5, 93, 101.5, 113, 122, 133.5) cm

13 1/4 (13 1/4, 16 1/2, 16 1/2, 16 1/2, 20) in/
33.5 (33.5, 42, 42, 42, 50.5) cm

6 (7, 8, 9, 10, 10, 10) in/
15 (18, 19.5, 22, 25.5, 25.5, 25.5) cm

11 1/2 (12, 12, 12 1/2, 13, 13 3/4, 14 1/2) in/
29.5 (30.5, 30.5, 31.5, 33, 34.5, 36.5) cm

40 (43 1/2, 48, 51 1/2, 56, 59 1/2, 64) in/
101.5 (110.5, 121.5, 130.5, 142, 151, 162) cm

Mother's Aran Coat

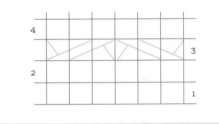

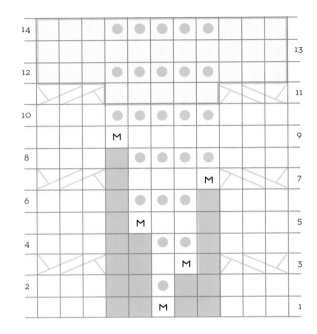

Baby's Cable Chart 1

- R1 (RS): k6
- R2 (WS): p6
- R3: c1 over 2 left, k1, c1 over 2 right
- R4: p6

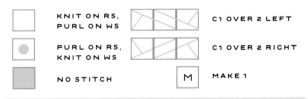

Baby's Cable Chart 2

- R1 (RS): k3, m1, k3
- R2 (WS): p3, k1, p3
- R3: c1 over 2 left, m1, k1, c1 over 2 right
- R4: p3, k2, p3
- R5: k5, m1, k3
- R6: p3, k3, p3
- R7: c1 over 2 left, m1, k3, c1 over 2 right
- R8: p3, k4, p3
- R9: k7, m1, k3
- R10: p3, k5, p3
- R11: c1 over 2 left, k5, c1 over 2 right
- R12: p3, k5, p3
- R13: k11
- R14: p3, k5, p3

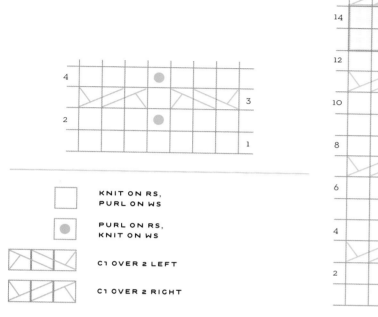

**KNIT ON RS,
PURL ON WS**

**PURL ON RS,
KNIT ON WS**

C1 OVER 2 LEFT

C1 OVER 2 RIGHT

Mother's Cable Chart 1

- R1 (RS): k7
- R2 (WS): p3, k1, p3
- R3: c1 over 2 left, k1, c1 over 2 right
- R4: p3, k1, c3

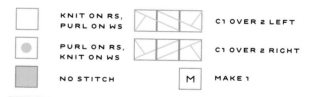

**KNIT ON RS,
PURL ON WS**

**PURL ON RS,
KNIT ON WS**

NO STITCH

C1 OVER 2 LEFT

C1 OVER 2 RIGHT

M MAKE 1

Mother's Cable Chart 2

- R1 (RS): k7
- R2 (WS): p3, k1, p3
- R3: c1 over 2 left, k1, m1, c1 over 2 right
- R4: p3, k2, p3
- R5: k3, m1, k5
- R6: p3, k3, p3
- R7: c1 over 2 left, k3, m1, c1 over 2 right
- R8: p3, k4, p3
- R9: k3, m1, k7
- R10: p3, k5, p3
- R11: c1 over 2 left, k5, m1, c1 over 2 right
- R12: p3, k6, p3
- R13: k12
- R14: p3, k6, p3
- R15: c1 over 2 left, k6, c1 over 2 right
- R16: p3, k6, p3

4

CLASSIC CARDIGAN

The mother's version of this cardigan combines a classic fit with simple raglan shaping to create a casual sweater that looks great with everything. The neckline, cuffs, and hem are accented with delicate leaves on a reverse stockinette stitch background.

The delicate baby version is knit using fingering weight yarn. The fiber content of the yarn (alpaca and merino wool) makes it a very soft option, and the viscose from bamboo means that it will hold its shape through many wearings. The yoke of the sweater is worked in garter stitch, with increases all worked on the right side rows. The body and sleeves are worked in stockinette, with a garter stitch trim. The leaf motif from the mother's version of the sweater appears as appliqués on the daughter's sweater yoke. Make as many appliqués as you like and stitch them wherever you want to add a little whimsy.

Baby's Classic Cardigan

MATERIALS

YARN

The Fibre Company Canopy Fingering (20% bamboo, 50% baby alpaca, 30% merino wool; 3.5-oz/100-g, 200-yd/ 91-m skein)

Plumeria, 1 (2, 2, 2, 2) skeins

NEEDLES

Size 2 (2.75 mm) 24-in/60-cm circular and DPN

NOTIONS

Six ¾-in/19-mm buttons

Darning needle

4 stitch markers of one color

8 stitch markers of a second color (for working charts)

2 stitch holders or lengths of waste yarn

GAUGE

32 sts and 44 rows per 4 in/10 cm worked in stockinette stitch on a US 2 (2.75 mm) needle

SIZES ◇ SHOWN IN SIZE: 6 MONTHS

SIZE (MONTHS)	3	6	12	18	24
TO FIT CHEST (IN)	16	17	18	19	20
TO FIT CHEST (CM)	40.5	43	45.5	48.5	51

FINISHED MEASUREMENTS

	3	6	12	18	24
CHEST CIRCUMFERENCE (IN)	18	19	20	21	22
CHEST CIRCUMFERENCE (CM)	45.5	48.5	51	53.5	56
LENGTH TO UNDERARM (IN)	7½	9	9	9½	10
LENGTH TO UNDERARM (CM)	19	23	23	24	24.5
TOTAL LENGTH (IN)	11¼	12¾	13½	14	15
TOTAL LENGTH (CM)	28	32.5	34.5	35.5	38

DIRECTIONS ◇

Yoke

- Using circular needle, CO 74 (74, 86, 96, 96) sts.

- Worked in garter stitch.

- Row 1 (WS): Knit, placing markers as follows: k14 (14, 16, 18, 18) for front, pm, k9 (9, 11, 12, 12) for sleeve, pm, k28 (28, 32, 36, 36) for back, pm, k9 (9, 11, 12, 12) for sleeve, pm, k14 (14, 16, 18, 18) for front.

- Row 2 (RS): [Knit to 1 st before m, kfb, slip m, kfb] 4 times, knit to end.

- Rows 3: Knit.

- Repeat the last 2 rows 20 (22, 23, 23, 25) times to 35 (37, 40, 42, 44) sts for each front, 51 (55, 59, 60, 64) sts for each sleeve, and 70 (74, 80, 84, 88) sts for back. 242 (258, 278, 288, 304) total sts.

Separate Sleeves from the Body

- Knit across front 35 (37, 40, 42, 44) sts, place next 51 (55, 59, 60, 64) sleeve sts on holder to be worked later, CO 2 (2, 0, 0, 0) sts at underarm, knit across 70 (74, 80, 84, 88) back sts, place next 51 (55, 59, 60, 64) sleeve sts on holder to be worked later, CO 2 (2, 0, 0, 0) sts at underarm, knit across front 35 (37, 40, 42, 44) sts. 144 (152, 160, 168, 176) body sts.

- Switch to St st and work even for 66 (77, 83, 88, 94) rows.

- Work in garter stitch for 20 rows.

- BO loosely.

Sleeves

- Transfer 51 (55, 59, 60, 64) sleeve sts from holder to DPN. Rejoin yarn and pick up and knit 2 (2, 0, 0, 0) sts CO at body underarm and work in St st for 56 (61, 78, 82, 82) rounds.

- Work in garter stitch for 10 rounds.

- BO loosely.

Leaf Appliqué

(see also Leaf Appliqué Chart on page 60)

- CO 5 sts

- Row 1 (WS): Purl.

- Row 2: K2 yo, k1, yo, k2 (7 sts).

- Row 3: Purl.

- Row 4: K2tog-tbl, k1, yo, k1, yo, k1, k2tog (7 sts).

- Row 5: Purl.

- Row 6: K2tog-tbl, k1, yo, k1, yo, k1, k2tog (7 sts).

- Row 7: Purl.

- Row 8: K2tog-tbl, k1, yo, k1, yo, k1, k2tog (7 sts).

- Row 9: Purl.

- Row 10: K2tog-tbl, k3 k2tog.

- Row 11: Purl.

- Row 12: K2tog-tbl, k1 k2tog.

- Row 13: Purl.

- Row 14: K3tog.

- Cut yarn and pull through last st on needle to bind off.

Button Bands

RIGHT FRONT

- With RS facing, and beginning at hem edge, pick up and knit 2 sts for every 3 rows over stockinette portion and 1 st for every 2 rows over garter stitch.

- Row 1 (WS): Knit.

- Row 2 (RS): Knit, evenly spacing 6 buttonholes along the row. Make each buttonhole by binding off 2 sts.

- Row 3: Knit, casting on 2 sts over the sts bound off for each buttonhole.

- Row 4: Knit.

- Bind off.

LEFT FRONT

- With RS facing, and beginning at left neckline edge, pick up and knit the same number of sts picked up for right front band.

- Work 4 rows in garter stitch.

- Bind off.

Finishing

- Weave in ends, attach buttons, attach leaf appliqués if desired.

Mother's Classic Cardigan

MATERIALS

YARN

The Fibre Company Canopy Worsted (20% bamboo, 50% baby alpaca, 30% merino wool; 3.5-oz/50-g, 100-yd/91-m skein)

Kaffir Plum, 9 (10, 12, 13, 15, 16) skeins

NEEDLES

Size 7 (4.5 mm) 24-in/60-cm circular and DPN

NOTIONS

Seven 1-in/2.5-cm buttons

Darning needle

4 stitch markers of one color

8 stitch markers of a second color (for working charts)

2 stitch holders or lengths of waste yarn

GAUGE

18 sts and 24 rows per 4 in/10 cm worked in stockinette stitch on US 7 (4.5 mm) needle

SIZES ◇   SHOWN IN SIZE: 34

SIZES	XS	S	M	L	1X	2X
TO FIT BUST (IN)	30	34	38	42	46	50
TO FIT BUST (CM)	76	86.5	96.5	106.5	117	127

FINISHED MEASUREMENTS

	XS	S	M	L	1X	2X
CHEST CIRCUMFERENCE (IN)	32½	36	40	44	48	52
CHEST CIRCUMFERENCE (CM)	82.5	91.5	101.5	112	122	132
LENGTH (IN)	24½	25	25	25½	26	26
LENGTH (CM)	62	63.5	63.5	65	66	66

DIRECTIONS ◇

Yoke

- Begin at the collar. The collar is worked in garter stitch, then the yoke is worked in reverse stockinette stitch with leaf motifs on the fronts and sleeves. Once the body and sleeves are divided, you will work in stockinette stitch. The hem and button bands are worked in garter stitch.

- CO 80 (80, 86, 86, 98, 98) sts.

- Knit 5 rows for garter stitch edging.

- Row 1 (WS): Knit, placing markers as follows: K15 (15, 16, 16, 18, 18), pm, k10 (10, 11, 11, 13, 13), pm, k30 (30, 32, 32, 36, 36), pm, k10 (10, 11, 11, 13, 13), pm, k15 (15, 16, 16, 18, 18).

- Row 2 (RS) *(see also Leaf Appliqué Chart on page 60)*: P11 (11, 12, 12, 14, 14) place chart marker, work leaf chart (starting on row 1 of the chart), place chart marker, kfb, slip m, kfb, place chart marker, work leaf chart, place chart marker, [purl to 1 st before m, kfb, slip m, kfb] twice, purl 6 (6, 7, 7, 9, 9), place chart marker, work leaf chart, place chart marker, kfb, slip m, kfb, place chart marker, work leaf chart, place chart marker, purl to end.

- Row 3 (WS): Knit, following leaf chart between chart markers.

- Row 4: Purl to chart marker, slip m, work chart, slip m, purl to 1 st before raglan marker, kfb, slip m, kfb, purl to chart marker, slip m, work chart, slip m, purl to 1 st before raglan marker, kfb, slip m, kfb, purl to 1 st before raglan marker, kfb, slip m, kfb, purl to chart marker, slip m, work chart, slip m, purl to 1 st before raglan marker, kfb, slip m, kfb, purl to chart marker, slip m, work chart, slip m, purl to end.

- Row 5: Knit, following leaf chart between chart markers.

- Repeat the last 2 rows 4 times to end of leaf chart. Remove chart markers. The remainder of the yoke will be worked in rev St st as follows:

- Row 1 (RS): [Purl to 1 st before m, kfb, slip m, kfb] 4 times, purl to end.

- Row 2 (WS): Knit.

- Repeat rows 1 and 2 14 (16, 17, 19, 19, 20) times to 36 (38, 40, 42, 44, 45) sts in each front, 72 (76, 80, 84, 88, 90) sts in back, and 52 (56, 59, 63, 65, 67) sts in each sleeve—248 (264, 278, 294, 306, 314) total sts.

Separate Sleeves from the Body

- Next row (RS): Removing all markers, knit across front 36 (38, 40, 42, 44, 45) sts, place next 52 (56, 59, 63, 65, 67) sleeve sts on holder to be worked later. CO 1 (5, 10, 15, 20, 27) sts using the backward loop method. Knit across back 72 (76, 80, 84, 88, 90) sts, place next 52 (56, 59, 63, 65, 67) sleeve sts on holder to be worked later. CO 1 (5, 10, 15, 20, 27) sts using the backward loop method, knit across front 36 (38, 40, 42, 44, 45)—146 (162, 180, 198, 216, 234) body sts.

Body

- The body is worked in stockinette, knitting on RS rows and purling on WS rows.

- Beginning with a purl row, work even (no increases or decreases) for 17 (15, 15, 13, 13, 13) rows.

- In the last row (WS), place side markers as follows: Purl 36 (40, 45, 49, 54, 58), pm, purl 74 (82, 90, 100, 108, 118), pm, purl 36 (40, 45, 49, 54, 58).

Waist Shaping

- Row 1 (RS): [K to 4 sts before marker, k2tog-tbl, k2, slip m, knit 2, k2tog] twice, knit to end.

- Rows 2-8: Work even in stockinette.

- Repeat rows 1-8 four times more—20 sts decreased. 126 (142, 160, 178, 196, 214) sts.

- Work even in St st (no increases or decreases) for 6 rows.

Hip Shaping

- Row 1: [K to 2 sts before marker, RLI, k2, slip m, k2, LLI] twice, k to end.

- Rows 2-4: Work even in St st.

- Repeat rows 1-4 four times more—20 sts increased. 146 (162, 180, 198, 216, 234) sts.

- Work even in St st for 6 (12, 12, 12, 12, 12) rows.

Begin Reverse Stockinette Stitch Border

- Work 12 rows in rev St st, beginning with a purl row.

- Work 10 rows in garter stitch.

- Bind off.

Sleeves

(make both the same)

- Transfer the 52 (56, 59, 63, 65, 67) held sleeve sts to DPN, rejoin yarn and knit across them; pick up and knit 1 (5, 10, 15, 20, 27) sts in the sts CO for the underarm and join to work in the round. Place a marker in the center of the underarm sts. 53 (61, 69, 78, 85, 94) sts.

- Work 9 (9, 9, 7, 7, 7) rounds even in stockinette.

- Next round: K2tog-tbl, k to last 2 sts, k2tog.

- Repeat these 10 (10, 10, 8, 8, 8) rounds 5 (7, 8, 9, 9, 9) more times. 66 (71 (72, 72, 72, 72) sts.

- Work even until sleeve measures 13 (14½, 15, 15¼, 15¼, 15¼) in/33 (37, 38, 39, 39, 39) cm, or 3 in/7.5 cm shorter than desired length.

- Work 14 rounds in rev St st (purl all rounds).

- Work 5 rounds in garter stitch (knit a round, purl a round).

- Bind off.

Button Bands

RIGHT FRONT

- With RS facing, and beginning at hem edge, pick up and knit 2 sts for every 3 rows.

- Rows 1 and 2: Knit.

- Row 3: K2, *BO 2 for buttonhole, k12, repeat from * 5 (5, 5, 6, 6, 6) more times, k to end of row.

- Row 4: Knit, casting on 2 sts over sts bound off for buttonholes.

- Rows 5 and 6: Knit.
- Bind off.

LEFT FRONT

- With RS facing, and beginning at left neckline edge, pick up and knit the same number of sts picked up for right front band.
- Work 6 rows in garter stitch.
- Bind off.

Finishing

- Weave in ends.
- Block.
- Attach buttons.

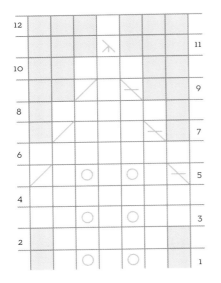

KNIT ON RS, PURL ON WS

NO STITCH

YO

K2TOG-TBL

K2TOG

SL1 K2TOG PSSO

(K1 P1 K1) IN 1 ST

Leaf Appliqué Chart

- R1 (RS): k1, yo, k1, yo, k1
- R2 (WS): p5
- R3: k2, yo, k1, yo, k2
- R4: p7
- R5: k2tog-tbl, k1, yo, k1, yo, k2tog
- R6: p7
- R7: k2tog-tbl, k3, k2tog
- R8: p5
- R9: k2tog-tbl, k1, k2tog
- R10: p3
- R11: sl1 k2tog psso
- R12: p1

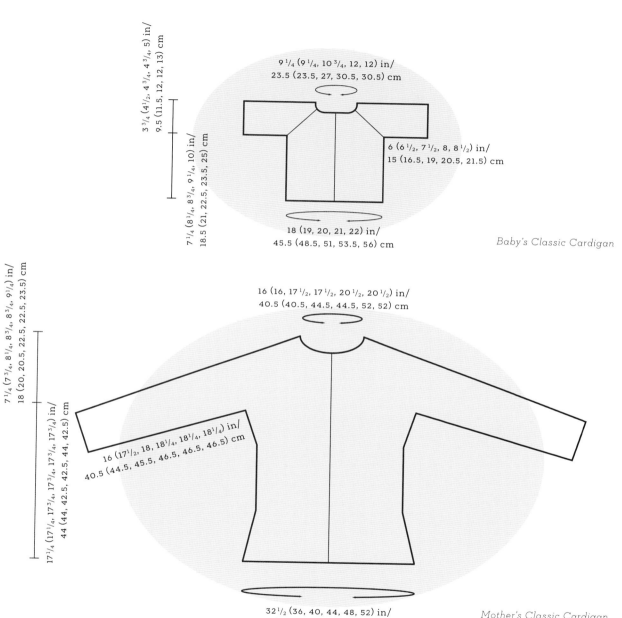

9 1/4 (9 1/4, 10 3/4, 12, 12) in/
23.5 (23.5, 27, 30.5, 30.5) cm

3 3/4 (4 1/2, 4 3/4, 4 3/4, 5) in/
9.5 (11.5, 12, 12, 13) cm

6 (6 1/2, 7 1/2, 8, 8 1/2) in/
15 (16.5, 19, 20.5, 21.5) cm

7 1/4 (8 1/4, 8 3/4, 9 1/4, 10) in/
18.5 (21, 22.5, 23.5, 25) cm

18 (19, 20, 21, 22) in/
45.5 (48.5, 51, 53.5, 56) cm

Baby's Classic Cardigan

16 (16, 17 1/2, 17 1/2, 20 1/2, 20 1/2) in/
40.5 (40.5, 44.5, 44.5, 52, 52) cm

7 1/4 (7 3/4, 8 1/4, 8 3/4, 8 3/4, 9 1/4) in/
18 (20, 20.5, 22.5, 22.5, 23.5) cm

16 (17 1/2, 18, 18 1/4, 18 1/4, 18 1/4) in/
40.5 (44.5, 45.5, 46.5, 46.5, 46.5) cm

17 1/4 (17 1/4, 17 3/4, 17 3/4, 17 3/4, 17 3/4) in/
44 (44, 42.5, 42.5, 44, 42.5) cm

32 1/2 (36, 40, 44, 48, 52) in/
82.5 (91.5, 101.5, 112, 122, 132) cm

Mother's Classic Cardigan

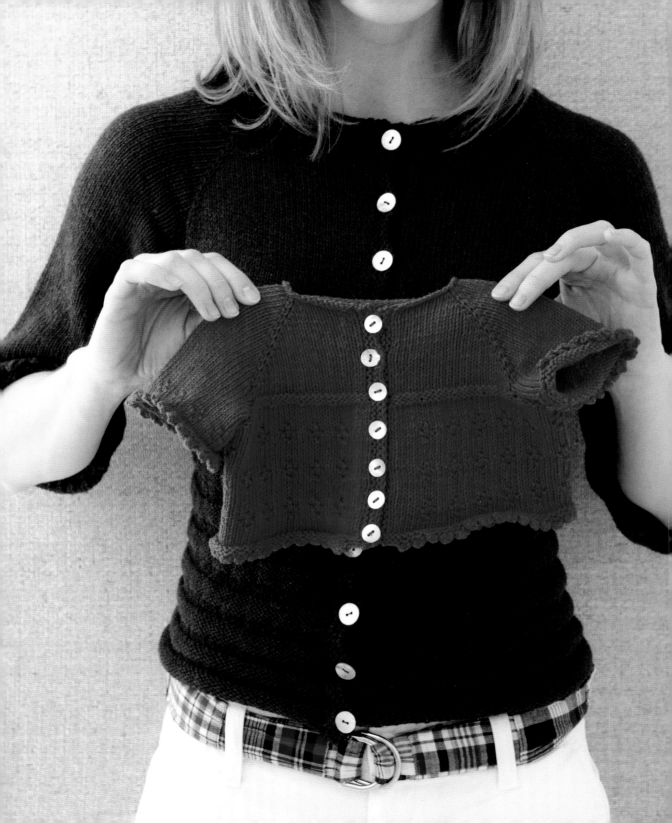

5

LADYLIKE CARDIGAN

I named this pair of sweaters "Ladylike Cardigans" because the picot edgings and fine cotton yarn make them the most feminine sweaters in this book. I chose to knit them in primary colors of organic cotton to tone down the girliness, but I think they'd look darling in pink as well. These cardigans are fancy enough for a special event, but rugged enough (thanks to washable cotton yarn) to wear every day.

Baby's Ladylike Cardigan

MATERIALS

YARN
Knit Picks Simply Cotton Sport (100% organic cotton; 164 yds/50 g)

Carnelian Heather, 2 (2, 2, 3, 3) skeins

NEEDLES
US 4 (3.5 mm) 24-in/60-cm or longer circular and DPN

NOTIONS
Seven ½-in/12.5-mm buttons

Darning needle

4 stitch markers

Stitch holders

GAUGE
24 sts and 30 rows per 4 in/10 cm

SIZES ◇ SHOWN IN SIZE: 6 MONTHS

SIZE (MONTHS)	3	6	12	18	24
TO FIT CHEST (IN)	16	17	18	19	20
TO FIT CHEST (CM)	40.5	43	45.5	48.5	51

FINISHED MEASUREMENTS

	3	6	12	18	24
CHEST CIRCUMFERENCE (IN)	18	18½	20	21¼	22
CHEST CIRCUMFERENCE (CM)	45.5	47.5	51	54	56
LENGTH (IN)	9	11	12½	15½	15¾
LENGTH (CM)	23	28	32	39.5	40

DIRECTIONS ◇

Yoke

- CO 48 (54, 64, 64, 64) sts.

- Row 1 (WS): Purl, placing markers as follows: 9 (10, 12, 12, 12) for front, pm, 6 (7, 8, 8, 8) for sleeve, pm, 18 (20, 24, 24, 24) for back, pm, 6 (7, 8, 8, 8) for sleeve, pm, 9 (10, 12, 12, 12) for front.

- Row 2 (RS): [K to 1 st before marker, kfb, slip m, kfb] 4 times, k to end.

- Row 3 and all odd rows: Purl.

- Repeat rows 2 and 3 12 (14, 15, 16, 17) times to 22 (25, 28, 29, 30) sts in each front, 32 (37, 40, 42, 44) sts in each sleeve, and 44 (50, 56, 58, 60) sts in back. 152 (174, 192, 200, 208) total sts.

Separate Sleeves from the Body

- Knit across 22 (25, 28, 29, 30) front sts. Place next 32 (37, 40, 42, 44) sleeve sts on holder to be worked later. Using the knit-on cast-on method, CO 10 (6, 4, 6, 6) sts at underarm, placing a marker to divide front from back. Knit across 44 (50, 56, 58, 60) back sts. Place next 32 (37, 40, 42, 44) sleeve sts on holder to be worked later. Using the knit-on cast-on method, CO 10 (6, 4, 6, 6) sts at underarm, placing a marker to divide front from back. 108 (112, 120, 128, 132) total body sts on the needle.

CREATE PURL BAND

- Next row (WS): Knit.

- Next row (RS): Purl.

- Increase row (WS): K2 (1, 0, 2, 1), *M1, k5* across to last 1 (1, 0, 1, 1) st, M1, k 1 (1, 0, 1, 1)—22 (23, 25, 26, 27) sts increased. 130 (135, 145, 154, 159) total sts.

- Next row (RS): Purl.

- Rows 1–5: Work 5 rows in stockinette, beginning with a WS (purl) row.

- Row 6 (RS): K5 (5, 5, 4, 4), repeat chart over next 120 (125, 135, 145, 150) sts, k5 (5, 5, 5, 5).

- Row 7: P5 (5, 5, 5, 5), repeat chart over next 120 (125, 135, 145, 150) sts, p5 (5, 5, 5, 4, 4).

- Rows 8–10: Continue as established in previous 2 rows.

- Repeat these 10 rows 2 (3, 4, 6, 6) more times. Work rows 1–5 once more.

Hemline Trim

- Row 1 (RS): Purl.

- Row 2 (WS): Knit.

- BO using picot bind-off as follows: BO 3, [knit 3 sts on, BO 5] to end. BO any remaining sts.

Sleeves

- Transfer 32 (37, 40, 42, 44) sleeve sts from holder to DPN.

- Knit across 32 (37, 40, 42, 44) sleeve sts, pick up and knit 10 (6, 4, 6, 6) sts in underarm. 42 (43, 44, 48, 50) sleeve sts.

- Knit in the round for 12 (15, 19, 22, 26) rounds.

Sleeve Stitch Pattern Detail

- Rounds 1–5: Knit 2 (3, 4, 3, 0) sts, work Mother and Baby Body and Sleeve Pattern Chart (on page 72) over 40 (40, 40, 45, 50) sts.

- Rounds 6–9: Knit.

Sleeve Trim

- Purl 2 rounds.

- BO using picot bind-off as for body.

Button Bands

RIGHT BUTTONHOLE BAND

- With RS facing, pick up and knit 2 sts for every 3 rows along right front.

- Row 1 (WS): Knit.

- Row 2 (RS): Knit, spacing 7 one-st buttonholes evenly along front. (*See techniques section.*)

- Row 3: Knit.

- Bind off.

- With RS facing, pick up and knit 2 sts for every 3 rows up left front.

- Knit 3 rows.

LEFT BUTTON BAND

- Bind off.

Finishing

- Weave in ends.

- Block.

- Attach buttons.

Mother's Ladylike Cardigan

MATERIALS

YARN
Knit Picks Simply Cotton Sport (100% organic cotton; 164 yds/50 g)

Prussian Heather, 6 (7, 7, 8, 9, 9) skeins

NEEDLES
US 4 (3.5 mm) 24-in/60-cm or longer circular and DPN

US 2 (2.75 mm) 24-in/60-cm or longer circular and DPN

NOTIONS
Ten 3/4-in/19-mm buttons

4 stitch markers

Darning needle

Stitch holders

GAUGE
24 sts and 30 rows per 4 in/10 cm

SIZES ◇ SHOWN IN SIZE: 34

SIZES	XS	S	M	L	1X	2X
TO FIT BUST (IN)	30	34	38	42	46	50
TO FIT BUST (CM)	76	86.5	96.5	106.5	117	127

FINISHED MEASUREMENTS

	XS	S	M	L	1X	2X
CHEST CIRCUMFERENCE (IN)	32½	36	40	44	48	52
CHEST CIRCUMFERENCE (CM)	83	91.5	101.5	112	122	132
LENGTH (IN)	20¼	20¾	22¼	22¾	24	24½
LENGTH (CM)	51.5	52.5	56.5	58	61	62

DIRECTIONS ◇

Yoke

- CO 96 (96, 120, 120, 132, 132) sts.

- Row 1 (WS): Purl, placing markers as follows: p18 (18, 22, 22, 24, 24) for front, pm, p12 (12, 16, 16, 18, 18) for sleeve, pm, p36 (36, 44, 44, 48, 48) for back, pm, p12 (12, 16, 16, 18, 18) for sleeve, pm, p18 (18, 22, 22, 24, 24) for front.

- Row 2: [knit to 1 st before m, kfb, slip m, kfb] 4 times, knit to end.

- Row 3: Purl.

- Repeat rows 2 and 3 26 (28, 29, 31, 31, 32) times. 312 (328, 360, 376, 388, 396) total sts.

Separate Sleeves from the Body

- Next row (RS): K across front 45 (47, 52, 54, 56, 57) sts, place next 66 (70, 76, 80, 82, 84) sts on holder to be worked later, CO 8 (14, 16, 24, 34, 42) sts at underarm, knit across back 90 (94, 104, 108, 112, 114) sts, place next 66 (70, 76, 80, 82, 84) sts on holder to be worked later, CO 8 (14, 16, 24, 34, 42) sts at underarm, knit across front 45 (47, 52, 54, 56, 57) sts. 196 (216, 240, 264, 288, 312) total body sts.

Body

- Next row (WS): Knit.

- Next row (RS): Purl.

- Increase row (WS): k3 (3, 0, 2, 4, 1) *M1, k10* across to last 3 (3, 0, 2, 4, 1) st, M1, k3 (3, 0, 2, 4, 1)—20 (22, 25, 27, 29, 32) sts increased. 216 (238, 265, 291, 317, 344) total sts.

- Work 4 rows in rev St st, beginning with a purl row.

- Row 1 (RS): K3 (4, 0, 1, 3, 2) sts, repeat pattern chart (see *Mother and Baby Body and Sleeve Pattern Chart on page 72*) over next 210 (230, 265, 290, 310, 340) sts, K3 (4, 0, 0, 4, 2).

- Row 2 (WS): P3 (4, 0, 0, 4, 2) sts, repeat pattern chart to last 3 (4, 0, 1, 3, 2) sts, p to end.

- Rows 3-5: Continue as established in previous 2 rows through the end of the chart.

- Rows 6-10: Work 5 rows in rev St st, knitting WS rows and purling RS rows.

- Repeat rows 1-10 8 (8, 9, 9, 10, 10) more times.

Hemline Trim

- Row 1 (RS): Purl.

- Row 2 (WS): Knit.

- BO using picot bind-off as follows: BO 3, (knit 3 sts on, BO 5) to end, BO last st if necessary.

Sleeves

- Transfer 66 (70, 76, 80, 82, 84) sleeve sts from holder to DPN.

- Round 1: Rejoin yarn and knit across 66 (70, 76, 80, 82, 84) sleeve sts, pick up and knit 8 (14, 16, 24, 34, 42) sts CO at body underarm. 74 (84, 92, 104, 116, 126) sleeve sts.

- Knit in the round for 68 (68, 75, 75, 83, 83) rounds (or to 2 in/5 cm short of desired length).

SLEEVE STITCH PATTERN DETAIL

- Rounds 1-5: Knit 4 (4, 2, 4, 1, 1) sts, work pattern chart over 70 (80, 90, 100, 115, 125) sts.

- Rounds 6-9: Purl.

SLEEVE TRIM

- Purl 2 rounds.

- BO using picot bind-off as for body.

Right Front Buttonhole Band

- With RS facing, pick up and knit 2 sts for every 3 rows along right front.
- Row 1 (WS): Knit.
- Row 2 (RS): Knit, spacing 10 one-stitch button-holes evenly along front. (*See techniques section.*)
- Row 3: Knit.
- Bind off.

Left Front Button Band

- With RS facing, pick up and knit 2 sts for every 3 rows up left front.
- Knit 3 rows.
- Bind off.

Neckline Trim

- With smaller needle, RS facing and beginning at right front neck, pick up and knit 1 st for every st cast on around neckline.
- Row 1 (WS): knit.
- Row 2: Knit.
- Bind off loosely.

Finishing

- Weave in ends.
- Block.
- Attach buttons.

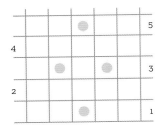

KNIT ON RS, PURL ON WS

PURL ON RS, KNIT ON WS

Mother and Baby Body and Sleeve Pattern Chart

- R1 (RS): k2, p1, k2
- R2 (WS): p5
- R3: k1, p1, k1, p1, k1
- R4: p5
- R5: k2, p1, k2

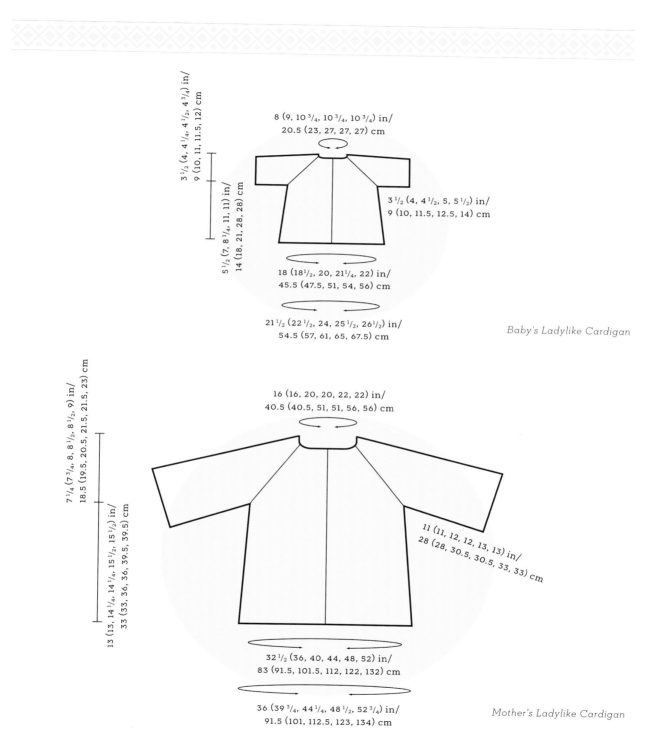

8 (9, 10 3/4, 10 3/4, 10 3/4) in/
20.5 (23, 27, 27, 27) cm

3 1/2 (4, 4 1/4, 4 1/2, 4 3/4) in/
9 (10, 11, 11.5, 12) cm

3 1/2 (4, 4 1/2, 5, 5 1/2) in/
9 (10, 11.5, 12.5, 14) cm

5 1/2 (7, 8 1/4, 11, 11) in/
14 (18, 21, 28, 28) cm

18 (18 1/2, 20, 21 1/4, 22) in/
45.5 (47.5, 51, 54, 56) cm

21 1/2 (22 1/2, 24, 25 1/2, 26 1/2) in/
54.5 (57, 61, 65, 67.5) cm

Baby's Ladylike Cardigan

16 (16, 20, 20, 22, 22) in/
40.5 (40.5, 51, 51, 56, 56) cm

7 1/4 (7 3/4, 8, 8 1/2, 8 1/2, 9) in/
18.5 (19.5, 20.5, 21.5, 21.5, 23) cm

11 (11, 12, 12, 13, 13) in/
28 (28, 30.5, 30.5, 33, 33) cm

13 (13, 14 1/4, 14 1/4, 15 1/2, 15 1/2) in/
33 (33, 36, 36, 39.5, 39.5) cm

32 1/2 (36, 40, 44, 48, 52) in/
83 (91.5, 101.5, 112, 122, 132) cm

36 (39 3/4, 44 1/4, 48 1/2, 52 3/4) in/
91.5 (101, 112.5, 123, 134) cm

Mother's Ladylike Cardigan

6

LIBRARY CARDIGAN

We love going to the library on a rainy day, and it's even more fun when we look the part of the bookish student. Knit from the top down, flat, on circular needles, this design incorporates increases at hip and sleeve to create a blouson effect for a modern silhouette. I-cord button loops are picked up and knit onto the sweater after finishing, and big, bold buttons add a bit of whimsy to this otherwise scholarly sweater.

Child's Library Cardigan

MATERIALS

YARN

Cascade 220 Heather (100% Peruvian highland wool; 3.5-oz/100-g, 220-yd/202-m skein)

Main color (MC): Color 9452, 2 (2, 2, 3, 3) skeins

Contrasting color (CC): Color 8908, 1 skein

NEEDLES

Size 7 (4.5 mm) 24-in/60-cm circular and double pointed needles (DPN), or size needed to match gauge

Size 5 (3.75 mm) 24-in/60-cm circular and DPN

NOTIONS

Six 1-in/25-mm buttons

Darning needle

4 stitch markers

2 stitch holders or lengths of waste yarn

GAUGE

18 sts and 24 rows per 4 in/10cm in stockinette stitch, using larger needle(s)

SIZES ◇ SHOWN IN SIZE: 8

SIZES	4	6	8	10
TO FIT (IN)	23	25	26½	28
TO FIT (CM)	58.5	63.5	68.5	71

FINISHED MEASUREMENTS

	4	6	8	10
CHEST CIRCUMFERENCE (IN)	23	25	27½	29¼
CHEST CIRCUMFERENCE (CM)	58.5	63.5	70	74.5
LENGTH TO UNDERARM (IN)	12½	13¼	14¾	15½
LENGTH TO UNDERARM (CM)	32	33.5	37.5	39.5
TOTAL LENGTH (IN)	18	19	21	22½
TOTAL LENGTH (CM)	45.5	48.5	53.5	57

DIRECTIONS ◇

Yoke

- Beginning at neck edge, using larger needle and MC, CO 40 (40, 48, 48) sts.
- Row 1 (WS): Purl, placing markers (pm) as follows: P1 for front, pm, p8 (8, 10, 10) for sleeve, pm, p22 (22, 26, 26) for back, pm, p8 (8, 10, 10) for sleeve, pm, p1 for front.

- Row 2: Kfb, slip m, [k2, LLI, knit across to 2 sts before m, RLI, k2, slip m] 3 times, kfb—8 sts increased; 1 each front, 2 each sleeve and back.

- Row 3 and all WS rows: Purl.

- Row 4: Kfb, kfb, slip m, [k2, LLI, knit across to 2 sts before m, RLI, k2, slip m] 3 times, kfb, kfb—10 sts increased; 2 each section.

- Row 6: Kfb, k1, RLI, k2, slip m, [k2, LLI, knit across to 2 sts before m, RLI, k2, slip m] 3 times, k2, LLI, k1, kfb—10 sts increased.

- Row 8: Knit to 2 sts before m, RLI, k2, slip m, [k2, LLI, knit across to 2 sts before m, RLI, k2, slip m] 3 times, k2, LLI, knit to end—8 sts increased.

- Row 10: Repeat row 8.

- Row 11: Repeat row 3.

- Repeat last 2 rows 10 (12, 13, 15) more times—164 (180,196, 212) sts; 18 (20, 21, 23) sts each front, 38 (42, 46, 50) sts each sleeve, and 52 (56, 62, 66) sts for back, end with a WS row.

Separate Sleeves from the Body

- Next row (RS): Knit across 18 (20, 21, 23) front sts, place next 38 (42, 46, 50) sleeve sts on holder, pm for underarm, knit across 52 (56, 62, 66) back sts, place next 38 (42, 46, 50) sleeve sts on holder, pm for underarm, knit across 18 (20, 21, 23) front sts—88 (96, 104, 112) sts for body.

Body

- Work even in St st until total length from cast on is 9$\frac{1}{2}$ (10$\frac{1}{2}$, 12$\frac{1}{2}$, 14) in/24 (26.5, 32, 35.5) cm, ending with a WS row.

Body Shaping

- Row 1 (RS): K4 (3, 2, 6), [M1, k10] across to last 4 (3, 2, 6) sts, M1, k4 (3, 2, 6)—97 (106, 115, 124) sts.

- Rows 2-10: Work even in St st.

- Row 11 (RS): K4 (3, 3, 2), [M1, k10] across to last 3 (3, 2, 2) sts, M1, k3 (3, 2, 2)—107 (117, 127, 137) sts.

- Rows 12-22: Work even.

- Row 23 (RS): K4 (4, 4, 4), [M1 k10] across to last 3 (3, 3, 3) sts, M1, k3 (3, 3, 3)—118 (129, 140, 151) sts.

- Rows 24-33: Work even.

- Row 34: Purl and increase 0 (0, 1, 2) sts or decrease 1 (0, 0, 0) sts evenly across—117 (129, 141, 153) sts for multiple of 6 sts+3.

Ribbing

- Change to smaller needles and work in 3x3 ribbing for 17 rows, beginning and ending first row with k3.

- BO loosely in ribbing.

Sleeves

- Transfer 38 (42, 46, 50) sleeve sts from holder to DPN, join and pm for beginning of round.

- Rounds 1–24: Work even in St st.
- Round 25: K4 (1, 3, 0), [M1, k10] 3 (4, 4, 5) times, M1, k4 (1, 3, 0). 42 (47, 51, 56) sts.
- Rounds 26–31: Work even.
- Round 32: K1 (4, 1, 3), [M1, k10] 4 (4, 5, 5) times, M1, k1 (3, 0, 3). 47 (52, 57, 62) sts.
- Work even for 10 (20, 25, 30) rounds.

NOTE: If you'd like to make a longer sleeve for more room to grow, work more rounds.

- Next round: K4 (0, 4, 0), [k2tog-tbl, k8] across to last 3 (2, 3, 2) sts, k2tog, k1 (0, 1, 0)—5 (6, 6, 7) sts decreased; 42 (46, 51, 55) sts remain.
- Work 3 rounds, decreasing 2 (2, 3, 3) sts on last round—40 (44, 48, 52) sts remain.
- Change to smaller needle(s) and work in 2x2 ribbing for 17 rounds.
- Change to CC and work in ribbing for 2 rounds.

NOTE: To create a fold-down cuff, work longer ribbing.

- BO loosely in ribbing.

Trim

- With RS facing, beginning at lower right front, and using smaller circular needle, pick up and k2 for every 3 rows up right front, 1 st for each st around CO at neckline, and 2 sts for every 3 rows down left front, taking care to pick up a multiple of 6+3 sts in order to work ribbing.

- Work in 3x3 ribbing for 18 rows.
- Change to CC, work 2 rows in ribbing.
- BO loosely in ribbing.

I–Cord Closures

- Using CC and smaller DPN, pick up and knit 3 sts in 3 knit sts of ribbed trim at right front. Work in I-cord for 12 rows (2 in/5 cm). Knit last row of I-cord together with the 3 sts from the knit section of ribbed trim to join (3 purls are between the two sections). Repeat for each button. Refer to garment photo for an example of loop placement, but feel free to add as many buttons as you like.

Pockets

(make 2)

- Using CC and smaller needle, CO 33 sts.
- Next row (RS): Work in 3x3 ribbing for 2 rows.
- Change to MC and continue ribbing for 12 more rows.
- Work even in St st for 10 rows, end with a WS row.

POCKET SHAPING

- Row 1 (RS): K2, k2tog-tbl, knit across to last 4 sts, k2tog, k2—2 sts decreased.
- Row 2: Purl.

- Repeat last 2 rows 4 more times—23 sts remain.
- Bind off.

Finishing

- Attach buttons to left front opposite button loops.
- Attach pockets as shown in photo, approximately 5 sts in from front edge and 10 rows up from the top of the ribbing.
- Weave in ends.
- Block or steam if desired, being careful not to flatten texture of ribbing.

Mother's Library Cardigan

MATERIALS

YARN
Cascade 220 Heather (100% Peruvian highland wool; 3.5-oz/100-g, 220-yd/202-m skein)

Main color (MC): Color 9410, 6 (7, 7, 8, 9, 9) skeins

Contrasting color (CC): Color 8908, 1 skein

NEEDLES
Size 7 (4.5 mm) 24-in/60-cm circular and double pointed needles (DPN), or size needed to match gauge

Size 5 (3.75 mm) 24-in/60-cm circular and DPN

NOTIONS
Seven 1-in/25-mm buttons

Darning needle

4 stitch markers

2 stitch holders or lengths of waste yarn

GAUGE
18 sts and 24 rows per 4 in/10cm in stockinette stitch, using larger needle(s)

SIZES ⬦ SHOWN IN SIZE: 34

SIZES	XS	S	M	L	1X	2X
TO FIT BUST (IN)	30	34	38	42	46	50
TO FIT BUST (CM)	76	86.5	96.5	107	117	127

FINISHED MEASUREMENTS

	XS	S	M	L	1X	2X
BUST (IN)	31	34½	40	44	48	52
BUST (CM)	79	88	101.5	112	122	132
LENGTH TO UNDERARM (IN)	19¼	20	20½	21	21¼	22¼
LENGTH TO UNDERARM (CM)	49	51	52	53.5	54	56.5
LENGTH TO SHOULDER (IN)	26¾	28	29	30	30¾	31¾
LENGTH TO SHOULDER (CM)	68	71	73.5	76	78	80.5

DIRECTIONS

Yoke

- Beginning at neck edge, using larger needle and MC, CO 47 (47, 56, 56, 64, 64) sts.

- Row 1 (WS): Purl, placing markers (pm) as follows: P1 for front, pm, p9 (9, 11, 11, 13, 13) for sleeve, pm, p27 (27, 32, 32, 36, 36) for back, pm, p9 (9, 11, 11, 13, 13) for sleeve, pm, p1 for front.

- Row 2 (RS): Kfb, slip m, [k2, RLI, knit across to 2 sts before m, LLI, k2, slip m] 3 times, kfb—8 sts increased.

- Row 3 and all WS rows: Purl.

- Row 4: Kfb, kfb, slip m, [k2, RLI, knit across to 2 sts before m, LLI, k2, slip m] 3 times, kfb, kfb—10 sts increased.

- Row 6: Kfb, k to 2 sts before marker, LLI, k2, slip m, [k2, RLI, knit across to 2 sts before m, LLI, k2, slip m] 3 times, k2, RLI, k to last st, kfb—10 sts increased.

- Rows 8-19: Repeat rows 6 and 7 six more times—135 (135, 144, 144, 152, 152) sts (18 sts for each front).

- Row 20: Knit to 2 sts before m, LLI, k2, slip m, [k2, RLI, knit across to 2 sts before m, LLI, k2, slip m] 3 times, k2, LLI, knit to end—8 sts increased.

- Row 21: Repeat row 3.

- Repeat last 2 rows 11 (13, 14, 16, 16, 17) more times—231 (247, 264, 280, 288, 296) sts; 30 (32, 33, 35, 35, 36) sts for each front, 51 (55, 59, 63, 65, 67) sts for each sleeve, 69 (73, 80, 84, 88, 90) sts for back.

Separate Sleeves from the Body

- Next row (RS): K30 (32, 33, 35, 35, 36) front sts, place next 51 (55, 59, 63, 65, 67) sleeve sts on holder, using the backward loop method CO 1 (5, 10, 15, 20, 27) sts for underarm, k69 (73, 80, 84, 88, 90) back sts, place next 51 (55, 59, 63, 65, 67) sleeve sts on holder, using the backward loop method, CO 1 (5, 10, 15, 20, 27) sts for underarm, k30 (32, 33, 35, 35, 36) front sts. 131 (147, 166, 184, 198, 216) sts for body.

Body

- Work even in St st until total length from cast-on edge is 13 1/4 (14 1/2, 15 1/2, 16 1/2, 17 1/2, 18 1/2) in/ 33.5 (37, 39, 42, 44, 47) cm, ending with a WS row.

Body Shaping

- Row 1 (RS): K6 (4, 3, 2, 4, 3), [M1, k10] across to last 5 (3, 3, 2, 4, 3) sts, M1, k to end—13 (15, 17, 19, 20, 22) sts increased, 144 (162, 183, 203, 218, 238) sts total.

- Row 2: Purl.

- Rows 3-11: Work even in St st.

- Row 12: K2 (1, 2, 2, 4, 4), [M1, k10] across to last 2 (1, 1,1, 4, 4) sts, M1, k to end—15 (17, 19, 21, 22, 24) sts increased. 159 (179, 202, 224, 240, 262) sts total.

- Rows 13-21: Work even.

- Row 22: K5 (5, 1, 2, 5, 1), [M1, k10] across to last 4 (4, 1, 2, 5, 1) sts, M1, k to end—16 (18, 21, 23, 24, 27) sts increased, 175 (197, 223, 247, 264, 289) sts total.

- Rows 23-58: Work even, while at the same time, on last row, inc 2 (0, 2, 2, 0, 2) sts, dec 0 (2, 0, 0, 3, 0) sts evenly across—177 (195, 225, 249, 261, 291) sts remaining; (a multiple of 6+3).

Ribbing

- Change to smaller needle and work in 3x3 ribbing for 24 rows.

- BO loosely in ribbing.

Sleeve

- Transfer 51 (55, 59, 63, 65, 67) sleeve sts from holder to DPN, pm, pick up and knit the 1 (5, 10, 15, 20, 27) cast-on sts at underarm—52 (60, 69, 78, 85, 94) sts total; join and work in the round.

- Rounds 1–50: Work even in St st.

- Round 51: K2 (10, 9, 8, 5, 4), [M1, k10] across to m, M1—6 (6, 7, 8, 9, 10) sts increased 58 (66, 76, 86, 94, 104) sts total.

- Rounds 52–63: Work even.

- Round 64: K8 (6, 6, 6, 4, 4), [M1, k10] across to m, M1—6 (7, 8, 9, 10, 11) sts increased. 64 (73, 84, 95, 104, 115) sts total.

- Work even for 19 (24, 27, 29, 29, 29) more rounds.

- Next round: K4 (3, 4, 5, 4, 5), [k2tog-tbl, k2tog, k6] around—12 (14, 16, 18, 20, 22) sts decreased. 52 (59, 68, 77, 84, 93) sts remaining.

- Work 3 rounds even, and on last round, increase 2 (0, 0, 1, 0, 0) sts or decrease 0 (1, 2, 0, 2, 3) sts evenly around. 54 (58, 66, 78, 82, 90) sts.

- Change to smaller needle and work in 2x2 ribbing for 17 rounds.

- Change to CC and work in ribbing for 2 rounds.

- BO loosely in ribbing.

NOTE: To create a fold-down cuff, work longer ribbing.

Trim

- With RS facing, beginning at lower right front, and using smaller circular needle, pick up and knit 5 sts for every 6 rows up right front, 1 st for each st around cast-on neckline, and 5 sts for every 6 rows down left front, taking care to pick up and knit a multiple of 6+3 sts for ribbing.

- Work in 3x3 ribbing for 18 (18, 24, 24, 36, 36) rows.

- Change to CC and continue in ribbing for 2 rows.

- BO loosely in ribbing.

I-Cord Closures

- See photo for an example of buttonhole placement. To create I-cord button loops, using CC, pick up and knit 3 sts from 3 knit sts in ribbed trim at right front. Work in I-cord for 12 rows (2 in/5 cm). Knit last row of I-cord together with next 3 knit sts of ribbed trim (3 purls are between the 2 sets). Repeat for each button loop.

Pockets

- Using CC and smaller needle, cast on 45 sts.

- Work in 3x3 ribbing for 2 rows.

- Change to MC and continue ribbing for 12 more rows.

POCKET SHAPING

- Row 1: Knit 2, k2tog-tbl, knit to last 4 sts, k2tog, k2.

- Row 2: Purl.

- Repeat rows 1 and 2 six times (seven total decrease rows).

- Bind off.

Finishing

- Attach buttons to left front, opposite button loops.

- Attach pockets approximately 5 sts in from front edge and 10 rows up from the top of the ribbing.

- Weave in ends.

- Block or steam if desired, being careful not to flatten texture of ribbing.

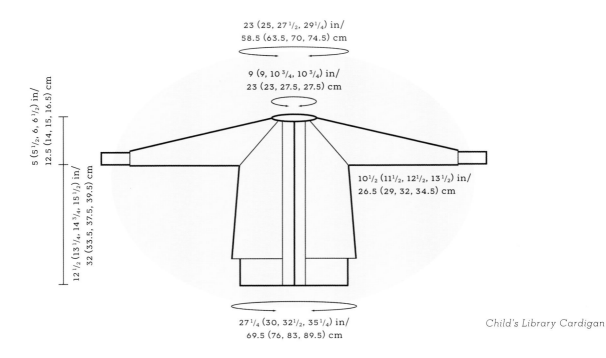

23 (25, 27$\frac{1}{2}$, 29$\frac{1}{4}$) in/
58.5 (63.5, 70, 74.5) cm

9 (9, 10$\frac{3}{4}$, 10$\frac{3}{4}$) in/
23 (23, 27.5, 27.5) cm

5 (5$\frac{1}{2}$, 6, 6$\frac{1}{2}$) in/
12.5 (14, 15, 16.5) cm

10$\frac{1}{2}$ (11$\frac{1}{2}$, 12$\frac{1}{2}$, 13$\frac{1}{2}$) in/
26.5 (29, 32, 34.5) cm

12$\frac{1}{2}$ (13$\frac{1}{4}$, 14$\frac{3}{4}$, 15$\frac{1}{2}$) in/
32 (33.5, 37.5, 39.5) cm

27$\frac{1}{4}$ (30, 32$\frac{1}{2}$, 35$\frac{1}{4}$) in/
69.5 (76, 83, 89.5) cm

Child's Library Cardigan

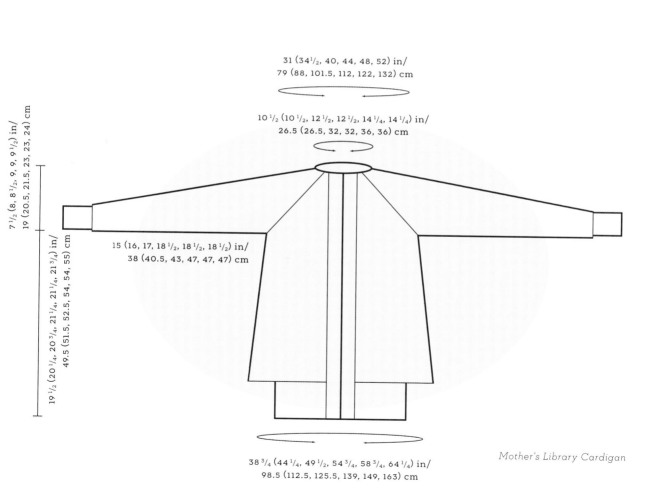

31 (34 1/2, 40, 44, 48, 52) in/
79 (88, 101.5, 112, 122, 132) cm

10 1/2 (10 1/2, 12 1/2, 12 1/2, 14 1/4, 14 1/4) in/
26.5 (26.5, 32, 32, 36, 36) cm

7 1/2 (8, 8 1/2, 9, 9, 9 1/2) in/
19 (20.5, 21.5, 23, 23, 24) cm

15 (16, 17, 18 1/2, 18 1/2, 18 1/2) in/
38 (40.5, 43, 47, 47, 47) cm

19 1/2 (20 1/4, 20 3/4, 21 1/4, 21 1/4, 21 3/4) in/
49.5 (51.5, 52.5, 54, 54, 55) cm

38 3/4 (44 1/4, 49 1/2, 54 3/4, 58 3/4, 64 1/4) in/
98.5 (112.5, 125.5, 139, 149, 163) cm

Mother's Library Cardigan

HALTER TOP

What little girl doesn't love cute, matching outfits? With this pair of sweaters, she and her favorite doll can match each other. Even better, this project is easy enough to be a mother-daughter team project: daughter can knit the little pieces for her doll's halter, and mom can do the seaming and finishing.

This top looks great worn alone or as a little vest over tees and turtlenecks. Believe it or not, this halter is a top-down raglan sweater. The front and back are cast on separately at the neckline, and each piece is worked individually to the bottom of the armhole. The front and back sections are then joined and worked in the round. The hemline is accented by a picot edge, where the hem is folded under and seamed.

Child's Halter Top

MATERIALS

YARN
Malabrigo Organic Cotton
(100% organic cotton;
3.5-oz/100-g,
230-yd/210-m skein)

Rosado, 2 (2, 2, 2) skeins

NEEDLES
US 5 (3.75 mm) 16-in/
40.5-cm circular

NOTIONS
Darning needle

Stitch markers

Stitch holders

Length of ribbon for ties

GAUGE
21 sts and 32 rows
per 4 in/10 cm

SIZES   SHOWN IN SIZE: 4

SIZES	4	6	8	10
TO FIT CHEST (IN)	23	25	27	28
TO FIT CHEST (CM)	58.5	63.5	68.5	71

FINISHED MEASUREMENTS

	4	6	8	10
CHEST CIRCUMFERENCE (IN)	25	27	29	30
CHEST CIRCUMFERENCE (CM)	64	68.5	73.5	76.5
LENGTH (IN)	15½	16½	17	18¼
LENGTH (CM)	39.5	42	43	46.5

DIRECTIONS

Front

- CO 25 (25, 27, 27) sts.

- Beginning with a purl row, work in St st for 5 rows.

- Row 6 (RS): Purl.

- Row 7 (WS): Purl.

- Work in St st 4 more rows.

- Begin raglan shaping. Setup row (RS): K3, RLI, k1 (1, 2, 2), place chart marker, work chart over next 17 sts, place chart marker, k to last 3 sts, LLI, k3.

- Row 1: k3, p to marker, work Lace Chart over next 17 sts, p to last 3 sts, k3.

- Row 2: k3, RLI, k to marker, work chart over next 17 sts, k to last 3 sts, LLI, k3.

- Repeat the last 2 rows 17 (19, 19, 21) times, then work row 1 once more.

- 63 (67, 69, 73) sts. Piece measures 4½ (5¼, 5¼, 5½) in/11.5 (13, 13, 14) cm from beginning of lace panel.

- Make note of last chart row worked. Do not cut yarn; place front section on a stitch holder to be worked later.

Back

- With second ball of yarn, work as front, omitting lace panel, leave the piece on the circular needle. Cut yarn.

Joining Front and Back to Work in the Round

- With RS facing, slide back section to the cable portion of the circular needle, and transfer front section to needle, also with RS facing. Yarn is ready to work a RS row.

- Knit across front to chart marker, continuing from where you left off in the Lace Chart, work chart over next 17 sts. Knit to edge of front section. Using the knit-on cast-on method, CO 3 (4, 7, 6) sts. Knit across back section, using the knit-on cast-on method, CO 3 (4, 7, 6) sts. Place marker to denote beginning of round. 132 (142, 152, 158) total sts.

- The halter is now worked in the round with no increases or decreases to hem, working Lace Chart between chart markers as established above. Now that you are working the chart in the round, remember to work lace operations on one round, and knit on the next.

- Work in this manner until piece measures 9.5 (10, 10.5, 11) in/24 (25.5, 26.5, 28) cm from underarm join.

Hem

- Foldover round: (k2tog, yo) to end.

- Work in stockinette for 6 rounds.

- BO very loosely.

- Fold hem under at foldover round and stitch to WS of halter.

Ribbon Casings at Neckline

- Fold neckline ribbon casings (top edge of halter) at purl ridge, and seam to WS of halter.

- Thread ribbons through casings.

Finishing

- Weave in ends.

- Block.

Doll's Halter Top

MATERIALS

YARN

Malabrigo Organic Cotton
(100% organic cotton;
3.5-oz/100-g,
230-yd/210-m skein)

Rosado, a few of the leftover
yards from the child's halter

NEEDLES

US 5 (3.75 mm) straight

NOTIONS

Darning needle

Stitch markers

Stitch holders

GAUGE

21 sts and 25 rows
per 4 in/10 cm

FINISHED MEASUREMENTS

CIRCUMFERENCE (IN)	5
CIRCUMFERENCE (CM)	12.5
LENGTH (IN)	2¾
LENGTH (CM)	7

DIRECTIONS

Front and Back

- Make 2 of the following pattern.
- CO 13 sts.
- Row 1 (RS): Knit.
- Row 2: Knit.
- Row 3: Knit.
- Row 4: Purl.
- Repeat rows 3 and 4 until piece measures approximately 2³⁄₄ in/7 cm.
- Knit 1 row.

- Bind off.

- With wrong sides together, seam $1\frac{1}{2}$ in/4 cm at each side, starting at cast-on edge.

- Seam a few sts at each shoulder.

OPTIONAL: Using a length of contrasting yarn, embroider the doll's halter to simulate the lace pattern on the child's halter, as indicated in the illustration, right.

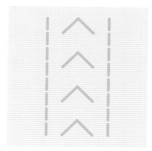

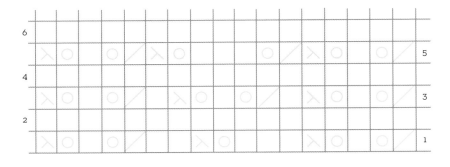

	KNIT ON RS, PURL ON WS
	YO
	K2TOG
	SKP

Lace Chart

- R1 (RS): k2tog, yo, k1, yo, skp, k3, yo, skp, k2, k2tog, yo, k1, yo, skp

- R2 (WS): p17

- R3: k2tog, yo, k1, yo, skp, k1, k2tog, yo, k1, yo, skp, k1, k2tog, yo, k1, yo, skp

- R4: p17

- R5: k2tog, yo, k1, yo, skp, k2tog, yo, k3, yo, skp, k2tog, yo, k1, yo, skp

- R6: p17

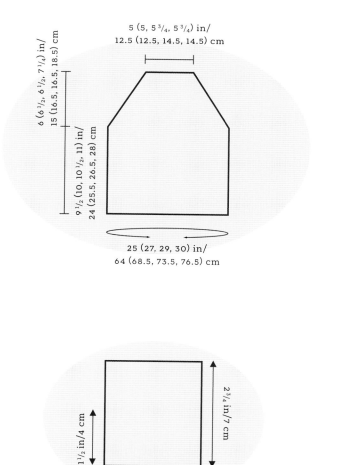

5 (5, 5 3/4, 5 3/4) in/
12.5 (12.5, 14.5, 14.5) cm

6 (6 1/2, 6 1/2, 7 1/4) in/
15 (16.5, 16.5, 18.5) cm

9 1/2 (10, 10 1/2, 11) in/
24 (25.5, 26.5, 28) cm

25 (27, 29, 30) in/
64 (68.5, 73.5, 76.5) cm

Child's Halter Top

2 3/4 in/7 cm

1 1/2 in/4 cm

2 1/2 in/6.5 cm

Doll's Halter Top

8

PUEBLA TOP

These tops are inspired by the beautifully embroidered "China Poblana" peasant tops from Mexico, known in the United States as "Puebla dresses." The examples shown here are very simply embroidered, but you can make yours as fancy as you like!

The top is knit in one piece from neckline to hem, with fluttery short sleeves and a button at the front neck. A picot bind-off creates contrasting lacy trim, and you can use a range of colors to embroider your motifs. Use scrap yarns for the embroidery if you have them, but please make sure that you use yarns of the same fiber content as that of the main yarn used for the top. This will ensure that there is no shrinkage when you wash your finished garments.

Child's Puebla Top

MATERIALS

YARN

LB Collection Cotton Bamboo (52% cotton, 48% bamboo; 3.5-oz/100-g, 245-yd/225-m skein)

Main color (MC): Hibiscus, 2 (2, 2, 3, 3) skeins

Contrast color (CC): Cherry Blossom, 1 skein, all sizes

Additional colors for embellishment as desired. Garments pictured used Cherry Blossom and Gardenia.

NEEDLES

US 6 (4 mm) 24-in/60-cm circular and DPN, or size needed to match gauge

US G-6 (4 mm) crochet hook (optional)

NOTIONS

Two ½-in/12.5-mm buttons

Darning needle

4 stitch markers

2 stitch holders or lengths of waste yarn

GAUGE

21 sts and 24 rows per 4 in/10 cm in stockinette stitch

SIZES ◇ SHOWN IN SIZE: 8

SIZES	4	6	8	10
TO FIT (IN)	23	25	27	28
TO FIT (CM)	58.5	63.5	68.5	71

FINISHED MEASUREMENTS

	4	6	8	10
CHEST CIRCUMFERENCE (IN)	24¼	25¾	27¼	29
CHEST CIRCUMFERENCE (CM)	62	66	69.5	73.5
TOTAL LENGTH (IN)	16½	20	21	23½
TOTAL LENGTH (CM)	42	51	53.5	59.5

DIRECTIONS ◇

Yoke

- Beginning at neck edge, using MC, CO 72 (72, 84, 84) sts.

- Row 1 (WS): Purl, placing markers as follows: P14 (14, 16, 16) for front, pm; p8 (8, 10, 10) for sleeve, pm; p28 (28, 32, 32) for back, pm; p8 (8, 10, 10) for sleeve, pm; p14 (14, 16, 16) for front.

- Row 2: Increase row (RS): P3 (edge sts), [knit to 1 st before m, yo, k1, slip m, k1, yo] 4 times, knit to last 3 sts, p3 (edge sts)—8 sts increased, 1 on each side of each marker.

- Row 3: Purl.

- Repeat last 2 rows 17 (19, 19, 21) times, maintaining edge sts in garter stitch (purl every row), ending with a WS row—216 (232, 244, 260) sts; 32 (34, 36, 38) sts each front, 64 (68, 72, 76) sts for back, and 44 (48, 50, 54) sts each sleeve.

Separate Sleeves and Join Body

NOTE: Pm at each underarm between front and back sts or mark center underarm st while working this row; left underarm marker becomes the beginning of round from this point on.

- K32 (34, 36, 38) front sts, place next 44 (48, 50, 54) sleeve sts on holder, pm for underarm, k64 (68, 72, 76) back sts, place next 44 (48, 50, 54) sleeve sts on holder, pm for underarm, k32 (34, 36, 38) front sts; join to work in the round—128 (136, 144, 152) sts for body. Knit to first marker at left underarm. This is now the beginning of round.

Body

- Rounds 1-3: Purl.

- Round 4: Knit.

- Round 5: Increase round: *K10, M1; repeat from * around to last 8 (6, 4, 2) sts, knit to end—12 (13, 14, 15) sts increased; 140 (149, 158, 167) total sts.

- Rounds 6-10: Knit even.

- Round 11: Increase round: *K10 M1; repeat from * around to last 0 (9, 8, 7) sts, knit to end—14 (14, 15, 16) sts increased; 154 (163, 173, 183) total sts.

- Knit even for 37 (55, 61, 73) rounds more, until piece measures 8 (11, 12, 14) in/20 (28, 30.5, 35.5) cm from underarm.

Trim

(also see Puebla Trim Chart on page 104)

- Change to CC.

- Round 1: Knit, decreasing 0 (1, 1, 1) sts—154 (162, 172, 182) sts.

- Rounds 2 and 3: Purl.

- Round 4: Knit.

- Round 5: *K2tog, yo; repeat from * around.

- Round 6: Knit.

- Rounds 7-11: Repeat rounds 2-6.

- Rounds 12 and 13: Repeat rounds 2 and 3.

- Rounds 14 and 15: Knit.

- BO using Picot bind-off method as follows: BO 3 sts, *CO 3 sts using knit-on cast-on method, BO 5 sts; repeat from * around, BO remaining sts.

Sleeves

(make 2)

- Transfer 44 (48, 50, 54) sts of one sleeve from holder to circular needle or DPN.

- Join for working in the round; pm for beginning of round at center of underarm.

- Round 1: Using MC, *(K5 M1); repeat from *
  around to last 4 (8, 0, 4) sts, knit to end—8 (8,
  10, 10) sts increased; 52 (56, 60, 64) sts.

- Using CC, work trim as for body.

Finishing

- Using crochet hook and CC, work a row of
  single crochet around neckline. Alternatively,
  pick up and knit 1 st for each st CO at neckline.
  Bind off.

- Using embroidery template as a guide, embellish the yoke of the top.

- Using crochet hook, join yarn at left front neck
  edge, ch 8 and sl st to garter edging $\frac{1}{2}$ in/1 cm
  down to create a button loop. Make 1 more button loop the same way halfway down the garter
  edging on the left side.

- Attach buttons to opposite edge of placket, in
  position directly across from the loops.

- Weave in all ends and block to measurements
  given. Round 1: Using MC, *(K5 M1); repeat from
  * around to last 4 (8, 0, 4) sts, knit to end—8 (8,
  10, 10) sts increased; 52 (56, 60, 64) sts.

- Using CC, work trim as for body.

Puebla Top Embroidery

These tops are embroidered using a darning or tapestry needle and yarn.

To create the border around the placket, embroider using the following steps:

To embroider the flowers, use duplicate stitch** to create the arrangement below:

You can use several different colors in one flower motif to switch up the looks of your flowers.

**Duplicate stitch: To work in duplicate stitch, simply thread yarn of the desired contrast color onto a darning or tapestry needle and use the contrasting yarn to mimic the look of actual knitting. Insert the needle from the WS of the fabric at the point of the V shape created by a knit stitch. Pull the yarn up through the fabric to the RS, behind the V of the stitch above, and then back down through the point of the V of the original stitch.

Mother's Puebla Top

MATERIALS

YARN

*LB Collection Cotton Bamboo
(52% cotton, 48% bamboo;
3.5-oz/100-g, 245-yd/225-m skein)*

*Main color (MC):
Persimmon, 3 (4, 4, 5, 5, 5) skeins*

*Contrast color (CC):
Cherry Blossom, 1 skein, all sizes*

*Additional colors for
embellishment as desired.
Garments pictured used Cherry
Blossom and Gardenia.*

NEEDLES

*US 6 (4 mm) 24-in/60-cm
circular and DPN, or size
needed to match gauge*

*US G-6 (4 mm) crochet hook
(optional)*

NOTIONS

Three ½-in/12.5-mm buttons

Darning needle

4 stitch markers

*2 stitch holders or lengths
of waste yarn*

GAUGE

*21 sts and 24 rows per 4 in/10 cm
in stockinette stitch*

SIZES ◇ SHOWN IN SIZE: 34

SIZES	XS	S	M	L	1X	2X
TO FIT BUST (IN)	30	34	38	42	46	50
TO FIT BUST (CM)	76	86.5	97	106.5	116	127

FINISHED MEASUREMENTS

	XS	S	M	L	1X	2X
BUST (IN)	32¾	34¼	38	42	46	50
BUST (CM)	83	87	97	106.5	116	127
TOTAL LENGTH (IN)	28½	29	29½	32	32½	32½
TOTAL LENGTH (CM)	72.5	73.5	75	81.5	82.5	82.5

DIRECTIONS ◇

Yoke

- Beginning at neck edge, using MC, CO 112 (112, 124, 124, 136, 136) sts.

- Row 1 (WS): Purl, placing markers (pm) as follows: p21 (21, 23, 23, 25, 25) for front, pm, p14 (14, 16, 16, 18, 18) for sleeve, pm, p42 (42, 46, 46, 50, 50) for back, pm, p14 (14, 16, 16, 18, 18) for sleeve, pm, p21 (21, 23, 23, 25, 25) for front.

- Row 2: Increase row (RS): P3 for garter stitch edging, [knit to 1 st before m, yo, k1, sl m, k1, yo] 4 times, knit to last 3 sts, p3 for edging— 8 sts increased; 1 each side of each marker.

- Row 3 (WS): Purl.

- Repeat last 2 rows 21 (23, 24, 24, 25, 26) times, ending with a WS row—288 (304, 324, 324, 344, 352) total sts; 43 (45, 48, 48, 51, 52) sts each front, 86 (90, 96, 96, 102, 104) sts for back, and 58 (62, 66, 66, 70, 72) sts each sleeve.

Separate Sleeves and Join the Body

- K43 (45, 48, 48, 51, 52) front sts, place next 58 (62, 66, 66, 70, 72) sleeve sts on holder, using the knit-on cast-on method, CO 0 (0, 4, 14, 18, 27) sts at underarm, placing a marker at the center of these sts, k86 (90, 96, 96, 102, 104) back sts, place next 58 (62, 66, 66, 70, 72) sleeve sts on holder, CO 0 (0, 4, 14, 18, 27) sts at underarm, placing a marker at the center of these sts, k43 (45, 48, 48, 51, 52 front sts—172 (180, 200, 220, 240, 262) body sts. Join to work in the round and knit to the left underarm marker; this now denotes the beginning of round.

Body

- Rounds 1–4: Knit.

- Round 5: Increase round: *K10, M1; repeat from * around to last 2 (0, 0, 0, 0, 2) sts, knit to end—17 (18, 20, 22, 24, 26) sts increased; 189 (198, 220, 242, 264, 288) total sts.

- Rounds 6–10: Knit.

- Round 11: Increase round: *K10 M1; repeat from * around to last 9 (8, 0, 2, 4, 8) sts, knit to end—18 (19, 22, 24, 26, 28) sts increased; 207 (217, 242, 266, 290, 316) sts total.

SIZES 30 AND 34 ONLY

- Knit even until piece measures 15 (16) in/ 38 (40.5) cm from underarm. Continue with trim.

SIZES 38–50

- Work bust darts using short rows as follows:

- Short row 1 (RS): Knit to 10 sts before left underarm marker, wrap next st and turn (w&t). Purl to 10 sts before right underarm marker, w&t.

- Short row 2: Knit to 6 sts before wrapped st, w&t. Purl to 6 sts before wrapped st, w&t.

- Repeat short row 2 for 1 (5, 8, 11) more times.

- Next row: Knit around, working wraps together with wrapped sts, and resume working in the round.

NOTE: Depending on your cup size, you may want to work more or fewer short rows for your bust darts; each set of 3 short rows adds 1 in/2.5 cm of depth at the front of the sweater.

- Knit even until piece measures 16 (16½, 17, 17) in/ 40.5 (42, 43, 43) cm from the underarm, measured along the side seam or down the back.

Trim (All Sizes)

(see also Puebla Trim Chart on page 104)

- Change to CC.

- Round 1: Knit, dec 1 (1, 0, 0, 0, 0) st(s)—206 (216, 242, 266, 290, 316) sts rem.

- Rounds 2 and 3: Purl.

- Round 4: Knit.

- Round 5: *K2tog, yo; repeat from * around.

- Round 6: Knit.

- Rounds 7-11: Repeat Rounds 2-6.

- Bind off.

Sleeves

(make 2)

- Transfer 58 (62, 66, 66, 70, 72) sts of one sleeve from holder to circular needle or DPN. Pick up and knit 0 (0, 4, 14, 18, 27) sts in the sts cast-on at underarm—58 (62, 70, 80, 88, 99) total sts.

- Using CC, work trim as for body, increasing 0 (0, 0, 0, 0, 1) st(s) on round 1.

Finishing

- Using crochet hook and CC, work a row of single crochet all around neckline.

- Alternatively, using CC, pick up and knit 112 (112, 124, 124, 136, 136) sts around neckline. Bind off.

- Using embroidery template as a guide, embellish the yoke of the top.

- Using crochet hook, join yarn at left front neck edge, ch 8 and sl st to garter edging ½ in/1 cm down to create a button loop. Make 2 more button loops the same way at 2-in/5-cm intervals down the garter edging on the left side.

- Attach buttons opposite loops.

- Weave in all ends and block to measurements given.

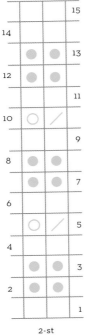

2-st
repeat

	KNIT ON RS, PURL ON WS
●	PURL ON RS, KNIT ON WS
○	YO
/	K2TOG

Puebla Trim Chart

- R1: knit 2
- R2: knit 2
- R3: purl 2
- R4: purl 2
- R5: k2tog, yo
- R6: purl 2
- R7: purl 2
- R8: knit 2
- R9: knit 2
- R10: yo, k2tog
- R11: knit 2
- R12: knit 2
- R13: purl 2
- R14: purl 2
- R15: knit 2

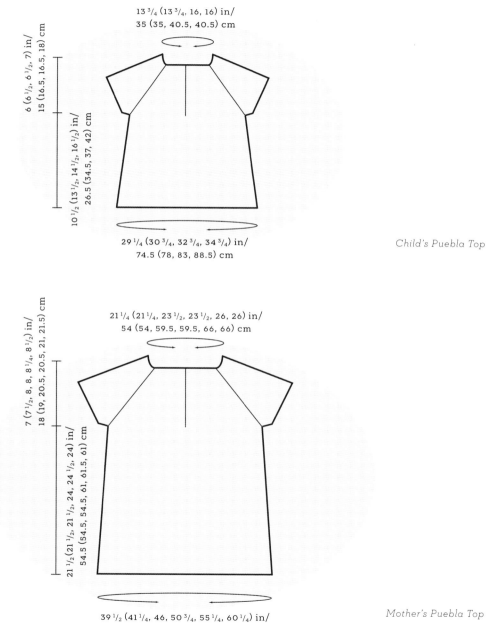

13 ¾ (13 ¾, 16, 16) in/
35 (35, 40.5, 40.5) cm

6 (6 ½, 6 ½, 7) in/
15 (16.5, 16.5, 18) cm

10 ½ (13 ½, 14 ½, 16 ½) in/
26.5 (34.5, 37, 42) cm

29 ¼ (30 ¾, 32 ¾, 34 ¾) in/
74.5 (78, 83, 88.5) cm

Child's Puebla Top

21 ¼ (21 ¼, 23 ½, 23 ½, 26, 26) in/
54 (54, 59.5, 59.5, 66, 66) cm

7 (7 ½, 8, 8, 8 ¼, 8 ½) in/
18 (19, 20.5, 20.5, 21, 21.5) cm

21 ½ (21 ½, 21 ½, 24, 24 ½, 24) in/
54.5 (54.5, 54.5, 61, 61.5, 61) cm

39 ½ (41 ¼, 46, 50 ¾, 55 ¼, 60 ¼) in/
100.5 (105, 117, 129, 140.5, 153) cm

Mother's Puebla Top

9

ARTIST'S VEST

These vests knit up quickly in bulky merino wool, and their clean lines and sawtooth edges give them a chic, unfussy look. Use a column of increases at each center front to create volume, shape the hem, and create flow in the fabric without adding bulk to the body of the vests.

Child's Artist's Vest

MATERIALS

YARN

*Malabrigo Chunky
(pure merino wool; 3.5-oz/
100-g, 100-yd/92-m skein)*

*Main color (MC):
Polar Morn, 3 (3, 3,
4, 4) skeins*

*Contrasting Color (CC):
Pearl Ten, 1 (1, 1, 1) skein*

NEEDLES

*Size 9 (5.5 mm)
24-in/60-cm circular,
or size needed to
match gauge*

NOTIONS

Crochet hook

Darning needle

4 stitch markers

GAUGE

*4 sts and 20 rows
per 4 in/10 cm worked in
stockinette stitch on
US 9 (5.5 mm) needle*

SIZES ◇ SHOWN IN SIZE: 4

SIZES	4	6	8	10
TO FIT CHEST (IN)	23	25	27	28
TO FIT CHEST (CM)	58.5	63.5	68.5	71

FINISHED MEASUREMENTS

	4	6	8	10
CHEST CIRCUMFERENCE (IN)	25	27	29	31
CHEST CIRCUMFERENCE (CM)	63.5	68.5	73.5	78.5
LENGTH (IN)	16¼	18	19	20½
LENGTH (CM)	41.5	45.5	48.5	52

DIRECTIONS ◇

Yoke

- CO 26 (26, 32, 32) sts.

- Row 1 (WS): Purl across, placing markers as follows: p2 (2, 2, 2) for front, pm, p3 (3, 5, 5) for sleeve, pm, p16 (16, 18, 18) for back, pm, p3 (3, 5, 5) for sleeve, pm, p2 (2, 2, 2) for front.

- Row 2: [K to 1st before m, kfb, slip m, kfb] 4 times, k to end.

- Row 3: Knit.

- Repeat the last 2 rows 5 (6, 6, 7) more times.

- Repeat row 2 once more. 9 (10, 10, 11) sts in each front, 17 (19, 21, 23) sts in each sleeve, and 30 (32, 34, 36) sts in back. 82 (90, 96, 104) total sts.

Cast Off Cap Sleeves

Next row (WS): P9 (10, 10, 11) right front sts, BO 17 (19, 21, 23) right sleeve sts, p30 (32, 34, 36) back sts, BO 17 (19, 21, 23) left sleeve sts, p9 (10, 10, 11) left front sts.

Place right front and back on stitch holders to be worked later. At this point, fronts and back are worked separately to desired armhole depth and then joined together to be worked back and forth in one piece to the hem.

Left Front

You will begin working center front increases every fourth row and, at the same time, increase at the armhole (the raglan line) every other row as follows:

Setup row (RS): k4, kfb, place marker, kfb, knit to last st on needle, kfb.

Rows 1 and 3 (WS): Purl.

Row 2: K to last st, kfb.

Row 4: K to 1 st before marker, kfb, slip m, kfb, k to last st, kfb.

Repeat rows 1–4 once (once, twice, twice) more. **Sizes 4 and 6 only:** Repeat rows 1-2 once more. 21 (22, 25, 26) sts.

Purl 1 WS row.

Put these sts on holder and transfer back sts to working needles.

Back

- Cut yarn and reattach to 30 (32, 34, 36) back sts, ready to work a RS row.

- Row 1 (RS): kfb, knit to last st, kfb.

- Row 2: Purl.

- Repeat these 2 rows 5 (5, 6, 6) times more. 42 (44, 48, 50) sts. Put these sts on hold and transfer sts for right front to working needles.

Right Front

- Cut yarn and reattach to right front, ready to work a RS row.

- Setup row (RS): kfb, k2 (3, 3, 4), kfb, pm, kfb, k4.

- Rows 1 and 3: Purl.

- Row 2: kfb, k to end.

- Row 4: kfb, k to 1 st before marker, kfb, pm, kfb, k to end.

- Repeat rows 1–4 once (once, twice, twice) more, **Sizes 4 and 6 only:** Repeat rows 1-2 once more. 21 (22, 25, 26) sts.

- Purl 1 WS row.

- Cut yarn and reattach to left front edge, ready to work a RS row.

- At this point, you will transfer all sections onto the circular needle, all aligned in the correct order, and with RS facing out.

Join Body

- You will continue the increases down the center of each front every fourth row as set.

- Transfer all sts back to working needle in the proper order with RS facing out.

- Reattach yarn at left front edge.

- Knit across left front, increasing at center front if necessary to maintain pattern, CO 1 (2, 2, 3) sts at underarm using the backward loop method, knit across back, CO 1 (2, 2, 3) sts at underarm using the backward loop method, knit across front, increasing at center front marker if necessary. 90 (96, 102, 108) sts.

- Row 1: Purl.

- Row 2: Knit, working increases at center fronts if necessary.

- Repeat these 2 rows, working center front increases every fourth row as established above, until piece measures 8 (9, 10 11) in/20 (23, 25.5, 28) cm or 2 in/5 cm less than desired total length.

Finish Body

- Work in garter stitch for 11 rows, continuing to increase at center front markers.

- Bind off.

Sawtooth Trim

- CO 7 sts.

- Row 1: k2tog, knit to end (6 sts).

- Row 2 and all even rows: Knit.

- Row 3: k2tog, knit to end (5 sts).

- Row 5: k2tog, knit to end (4 sts).

- Row 7: k2tog, knit to end (3 sts).

- Row 9: Slip 1, yo, knit to end (4 sts).

- Row 11: Slip 1, yo, knit to end (5 sts).

- Row 13: Slip 1, yo, knit to end (6 sts).

- Row 15: Slip 1, yo, knit to end (7 sts).

- Row 16: Knit.

- Repeat these 16 rows 12 (12, 13, 13) more times, to create 11 (11, 12, 12) full triangles, with one half triangle at each end.

NOTE: As the border is stitched to the front of the sweater, take care to:

- Line up the rows of garter stitch in trim and in the vest so that the border feels like an organic extension of the body edging.

- Stitch the pieces together carefully, so that each row of the trim lines up with a row from the body of the vest. (You don't have to sew into each stitch, but they should be aligned.)

- Center the back neck onto either the center point of one triangle (larger sizes) or the center point between two triangles (smaller sizes).

Finishing

- Weave in ends.

- Work a row of single crochet all around the armholes.

- Alternatively, pick up and knit one round around the armholes, BO.

- When blocking, you may wish to use a steam iron and gently tug the garter stitch trim at the bottom edge of the sweater to open it up and to clearly define the points formed by the shaping at each front marker.

Mother's Artist's Vest

MATERIALS

YARN

Malabrigo Chunky
(pure merino wool; 3.5-oz/
100-g, 100-yd/92-m skein)

Main color (MC):
Polar Morn, 4 (5, 5, 5, 6, 6)
skeins

Contrasting color (CC):
Pearl Ten, 1 (1, 1, 2, 2, 2)
skeins

NEEDLES
Size 9 (5.5 mm)
24-in/60-cm circular,
or size needed to
match gauge

NOTIONS
Crochet hook

Darning needle

4 stitch markers

GAUGE
4 sts and 20 rows per
4 in/10 cm worked in
stockinette stitch on
US 9 (5.5 mm) needle

SIZES ◇ SHOWN IN SIZE: 34

SIZES	XS	S	M	L	1X	2X
TO FIT BUST (IN)	30	34	38	42	46	50
TO FIT BUST (CM)	76	86.5	96.5	106.5	117	127

FINISHED MEASUREMENTS

	XS	S	M	L	1X	2X
CHEST CIRCUMFERENCE (IN)	32	36½	40	44½	48	52½
CHEST CIRCUMFERENCE (CM)	81.5	92.5	101.5	113	122	133.5
LENGTH (IN)	21	21½	21¾	23½	23½	24
LENGTH (CM)	53.5	54.5	55	59.5	59.5	61

DIRECTIONS ◇

Yoke

- CO 34 (38, 38, 38, 46, 46) sts.

- Setup row (WS): Purl, placing markers as follows: p2 (2, 2, 2, 2, 2) for front, pm, p7 (7, 7, 7, 9, 9) for sleeve, pm, p16 (20, 20, 20, 24, 24) for back, pm, p7 (7, 7, 7, 9, 9) for sleeve, pm, p2 (2, 2, 2, 2, 2) for front.

- Row 1: [Knit to 1 st before m, kfb, slip, kfb] 4 times, k to end.

- Row 2: Purl.

- Repeat these 2 rows 7 (7, 8, 9, 9, 9) more times.

- Repeat row 1 one more time. 11 (11, 12, 13, 13, 13) sts in each front, 25 (25, 27, 29, 31, 31) sts in each sleeve, and 34 (38, 40, 42, 46, 46) sts in back. 106 (110, 118, 126, 134, 134) sts.

Cast Off Cap Sleeve

- Purl across 11 (11, 12, 13, 13, 13) right front sts, BO 25 (25, 27, 29, 31, 31) right sleeve sts, purl across 34 (38, 40, 42, 46, 46) back sts, BO 25 (25, 27, 29, 31, 31) left sleeve sts, purl across 11 (11, 12, 13, 13, 13) left front sts.

- Place right front and back on stitch holders to be worked later. At this point, fronts and back are worked separately to desired armhole depth and then joined to be worked in one piece to the hem.

Left Front

- Begin working center front increases every fourth row and increase at armhole edge every other row as follows:

- Setup row: (RS): K4, kfb, place m, kfb, k across to last st on needle, kfb.

- Row 1 and 3 (WS): Purl.

- Row 2: K to last st, kfb.

- Row 4: K to 1 st before m, kfb, slip m, kfb, knit to last st, kfb.

- Repeat these 4 rows 3 (3, 3, 3, 4, 4) more times, then work rows 1 and 2 only 0 (1, 1, 1, 0, 1) times.

- Purl 1 WS row. 31 (32, 33, 34, 37, 38) sts.

- Work section as established above (working raglan increases every RS row and center front increases every fourth row) to a total of 35 (37, 39, 41, 43, 45) rows from cast-on edge.

Back

- Cut yarn and reattach to back section, ready to work a RS row.

- Row 1 (RS): kfb, knit to last st, kfb.

- Row 2: Purl.

- Repeat these 2 rows 8 (9, 9, 9, 10, 11) more times. 52 (58, 60, 62, 68, 70) sts.

Right Front

- Setup row: (RS): kfb, k4 (4, 5, 6, 6, 6) kfb, pm, kfb, knit to end.

- Row 1 and 3 (WS): Purl.

- Row 2: K to last st, kfb.

- Row 4: K to 1 st before m, kfb, slip m, kfb, knit to last st, kfb.

- Repeat these 4 rows 3 (3, 3, 3, 4, 4) more times, then work rows 1 and 2 only 0 (1, 1, 1, 0, 1) times.

- Purl 1 WS row. 31 (32, 33, 34, 37, 38) sts.

Body

- Transfer all sections to the working needle in the correct order with RS facing out. Reattach yarn to left front edge, ready to work a RS row. You will continue to increase at the front markers every fourth row as established.

- Setup row (RS): Knit across left front, increasing at center front marker if necessary. CO 2 (3, 6, 11, 13, 17) sts at underarm, using the backward loop method. Knit across back, placing a marker at center back; CO 2 (3, 6, 11, 13, 17) sts at underarm, using the backward loop method; knit across front, increasing at center front marker if necessary.

- Row 1: Purl.

- Row 2: Knit, working increases at center fronts if necessary.

- Continue as established until piece measures for 2 in/5 cm from underarm join, ending with a WS row.

- Continuing to work increases at center fronts as established, and, at the same time:

WORK WAIST DECREASES

- Row 1: K to 2 sts before center back marker, k2tog-tbl, sm, k2tog, k to end of row.

- Row 2: Purl.

- Row 3: Knit.

- Row 4: Purl.

- Repeat rows 1–4 3 more times. 8 sts decreased.

- Work 4 rows even.

WORK WAIST INCREASES

- Row 1: K to center back marker, LLI, sm, RLI, k to end.

- Row 2: Purl.

- Repeat rows 1 and 2 three more times. 8 sts increased.

Finish Body

- Continue as established for 12 (12, 12, 16, 16, 16) rows. Vest measures 10 (10, 10, 11, 11, 11) in/25.5 (25.5, 25.5, 28, 28, 28) cm from underarm.

- Change to CC and work in garter stitch for 19 rows, continuing to increase at center front markers.

- Bind off.

Sawtooth Trim

- With CC, CO 10 sts.

- Row 1 and all odd rows: Knit.

- Row 2: k2tog, knit to end (9 sts).

- Row 4: k2tog, knit to end (8 sts).

- Row 6: k2tog, knit to end (7 sts).

- Row 8: k2tog, knit to end (6 sts).

- Row 10: k2tog, knit to end (5 sts).

- Row 12: k2tog, knit to end (4 sts).

- Row 14: k2tog, knit to end (3 sts).

- Row 16: slip 1, yo, knit to end (4 sts).

- Row 18: slip 1, yo, knit to end (5 sts).

- Row 20: slip 1, yo, knit to end (6 sts).

- Row 22: slip 1, yo, knit to end (7 sts).

- Row 24: slip 1, yo, knit to end (8 sts).

- Row 26: slip 1, yo, knit to end (9 sts).

- Row 28: slip 1, yo, knit to end (10 sts).

- Repeat rows 1-28 a total of 9 (9, 9, 10, 10, 10) times, to create a total of 10 (10, 10, 11, 11, 11) points. 8 (8, 8, 9, 9, 9) full triangles, with one half triangle at each end.

NOTE: As the border is stitched to the front of the sweater, take care to:

- *Line up the rows of garter stitch in trim and in the vest, so that the border feels like an organic extension of the body edging.*

- *Stitch the pieces together carefully, so that each row of the trim lines up with a row from the body of the vest. (You don't have to sew into each stitch, but they should be aligned.)*

- *Center the back neck onto either the center point of one triangle (larger sizes) or the center point between two triangles (smaller sizes).*

Finishing

- Weave in ends.

- Using CC, work a row of single crochet all around the armholes.

- Alternatively, using CC, pick up and knit one round around the armholes, BO.

- When blocking, you may wish to use a steam iron and gently tug the garter stitch trim at the bottom edge of the sweater to open it up and to clearly define the points formed by the shaping at each front marker.

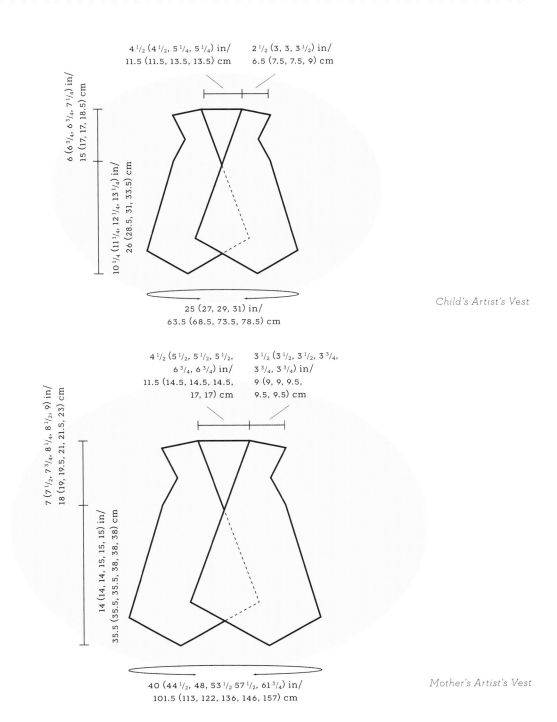

4 1/2 (4 1/2, 5 1/4, 5 1/4) in/
11.5 (11.5, 13.5, 13.5) cm

2 1/2 (3, 3, 3 1/2) in/
6.5 (7.5, 7.5, 9) cm

6 (6 3/4, 6 3/4, 7 1/4) in/
15 (17, 17, 18.5) cm

10 1/4 (11 1/4, 12 1/4, 13 1/4) in/
26 (28.5, 31, 33.5) cm

25 (27, 29, 31) in/
63.5 (68.5, 73.5, 78.5) cm

Child's Artist's Vest

4 1/2 (5 1/2, 5 1/2, 5 1/2,
6 3/4, 6 3/4) in/
11.5 (14.5, 14.5, 14.5,
17, 17) cm

3 1/2 (3 1/2, 3 1/2, 3 3/4,
3 3/4, 3 3/4) in/
9 (9, 9, 9.5,
9.5, 9.5) cm

7 (7 1/2, 7 3/4, 8 1/4, 8 1/2, 9) in/
18 (19, 19.5, 21, 21.5, 23) cm

14 (14, 14, 15, 15, 15) in/
35.5 (35.5, 35.5, 38, 38, 38) cm

40 (44 1/2, 48, 53 1/2 57 1/2, 61 3/4) in/
101.5 (113, 122, 136, 146, 157) cm

Mother's Artist's Vest

SHAWLETTE AND SCARF

A "shawlette" is a little shawl worn loosely draped around the neck like a scarf.

I have two daughters and neither one of them would wear a shawl because they are so young, but they do wear scarves. I created a keyhole version because I can put it on my one-year old, and she can't figure out how to remove it. If the little girl in your life is a knitter, she can even knit the garter stitch portion of the scarf herself!

Mother's Shawlette

MATERIALS

YARN
Malabrigo Merino Worsted (100% Merino Wool, 3.5-oz/100-g, 215-yd/ 197-m skein)

Ravelry Red, 2 skeins

NEEDLES
US 7 (4.5 mm) 24-in/60-cm circular

NOTIONS
Stitch markers

Darning needle

GAUGE
18 sts and 32 rows per 4 in/10 cm in stockinette stitch, blocked

DIRECTIONS

Garter Stitch Insert

- CO 3 sts.
- Knit 6 rows.
- Turn work 90 degrees and pick up 3 sts along garter stitch edge.
- Turn work 90 degrees and pick up 3 sts from cast-on edge.
- 9 sts.

Begin Shaping Shawl

- Row 1 (WS): k3, p3, k3.
- Row 2: k3, place m, yo, k1, yo, place m, k1, place m, yo, k1, yo, place m, k3 (13 sts).
- Row 3: k3, p7, k3.
- Row 4: k3, slip m, yo, knit 3, yo, slip m, knit 1, slip m, yo, knit 3, yo, slip m, knit 3 (17 sts).
- Row 5: k3, p11, k3.
- Row 6: k3, slip m, yo, knit to m, yo, slip m, knit 1, slip m, yo, knit to next m, yo, slip m, knit 3.
- Row 7: Knit 3, purl to last 3 sts, knit 3.

- Repeat rows 6 and 7 47 times, to 101 sts in each section between markers. (209 total sts.)

- Begin working Shawlette Chart on page 124.

- Repeat chart 3 times.

- BO loosely.

Finishing

- Weave in ends.

- Block.

Child's Scarf

MATERIALS

YARN
Malabrigo Merino Worsted (100% Merino Wool, 3.5-oz/100-g, 215-yd/ 197-m skein)

Ravelry Red, 1 skein

NEEDLES
US 8 (5 mm) any length straight or circular

NOTIONS
Stitch markers

Darning needle

GAUGE
20 sts and 32 rows per 4 in/10cm in garter stitch

DIRECTIONS

Left Side
- CO 15 sts and work in garter stitch for 39 rows.
- Work keyhole:
- Row 1: K5, BO 5, k5.
- Row 2: K5, using the "knitting on" method, CO 5 sts, k5.
- Work in garter stitch 6 more rows.
- Begin Scarf Chart on page 126. Work rows 1–33 once.
- BO by cutting yarn and pulling tail through last st.

Right Side
- CO 15 sts and work in garter stitch for 47 rows.
- Begin Scarf Chart. Work rows 1–33 once.
- BO by cutting yarn and pulling tail through last st.

Finishing
- Seam pieces together at CO edges, being sure that right sides are both facing out.
- Weave in ends.
- Block if desired.

KNIT ON RS, PURL ON WS
YO
K2TOG
SL1 K2TOG PSSO
K2TOG-TBL
PURL ON RS, KNIT ON WS

Shawlette Chart

- R1 (RS): yo, k1, yo, k3, sl1 k2tog psso, k3, yo, k1, yo, k3, sl1 k2tog psso, k3, yo, k1, yo

- R2 (WS): p23

- R3: yo, k2tog-tbl, k1, yo, k2, sl1 k2tog psso, k2, yo, k1, p1, k1, yo, k2, sl1 k2tog psso, k2, yo, k1, k2tog, yo

- R4: p23

- R5: yo, k2tog-tbl, k2, yo, k1, sl1 k2tog psso, k1, yo, k2, p1, k2, yo, k1, sl1 k2tog psso, k1, yo, k2, k2tog, yo

- R6: p23

- R7: yo, k2tog-tbl, k3, yo, sl1 k2tog psso, yo, k3, p1, k3, yo, sl1 k2tog, yo, k3, k2tog, yo

- R8: p23

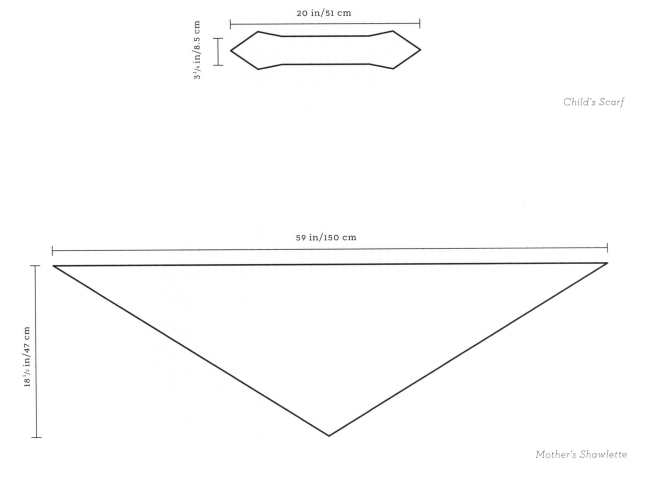

20 in/51 cm

3 1/4 in/8.5 cm

Child's Scarf

59 in/150 cm

18 1/2 in/47 cm

Mother's Shawlette

	KNIT ON RS, PURL ON WS
	YO
	K2TOG
	SL1 K2TOG PSSO
	K2TOG-TBL
	PURL ON RS, KNIT ON WS
	NO STITCH

Scarf Chart

- R1 (RS): k7, yo, k1, yo, k7
- R2 (WS): k5, p7, k5
- R3: k8, yo, k1, yo, k8
- R4: k5, p9, k5
- R5: k9, yo, k1, yo, k9
- R6: k5, p11, k5
- R7: k4, k2tog, k4, yo, k1, yo, k4, k2tog-tbl, k4
- R8: k4, p13, k4
- R9: k3, k2tog, k5, yo, k1, yo, k5, k2tog, k3
- R10: k3, p15, k3
- R11: k3, k2tog-tbl, k5, yo, k1, yo, k5, k2tog, k3
- R12: k3, p15, k3
- R13: k3, k2tog-tbl, k5, yo, k1, yo, k5, k2tog, k3
- R14: k3, p15, k3
- R15: k3, k2tog-tbl, k11, k2tog, k3
- R16: k3, p13, k3
- R17: k3, k2tog-tbl, k9, k2tog, k3
- R18: k3, p11, k3
- R19: k3, k2tog-tbl, k7, k2tog, k3
- R20: k3, p9, k3
- R21: k3, k2tog-tbl, k5, k2tog, k3
- R22: k3, p7, k3
- R23: k3, k2tog-tbl, k3, k2tog, k3
- R24: k3, p5, k3
- R25: k3, k2tog-tbl, k1, k2tog, k3
- R26: k3, p3, k3
- R27: k3, sl1 k2tog psso, k3
- R28: k3, p1, k3
- R29: k2, sl1 k2tog psso, k2
- R30: k5
- R31: k1, sl1 k2tog psso, k1
- R32: k3
- R33: sl1 k2tog psso

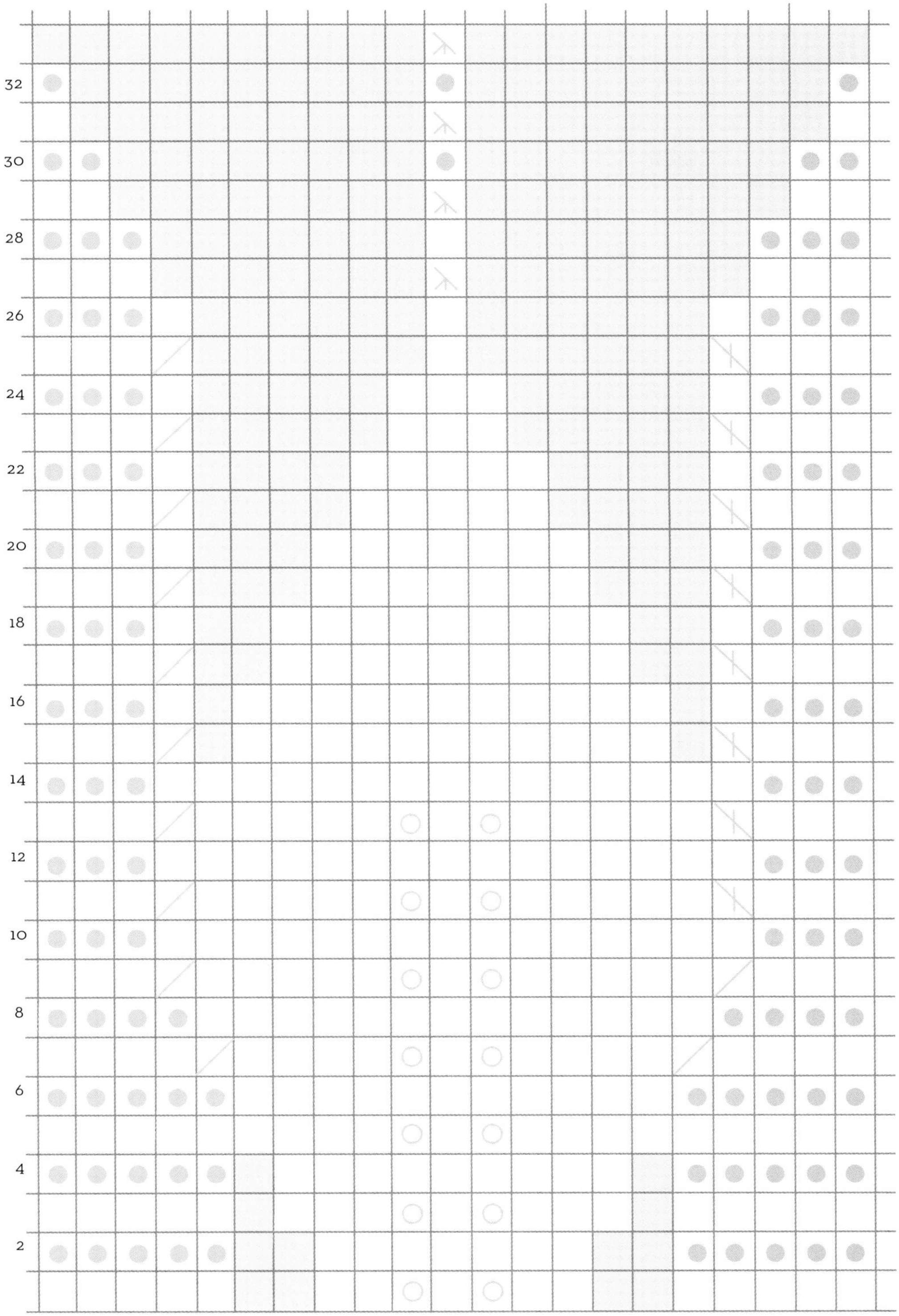
32
30
28
26
24
22
20
18
16
14
12
10
8
6
4
2

Resources

Yarn

Artfibers
266 Sutter Street, Third Floor
San Francisco, CA 94108
888-326-1112
www.artfibers.com/index.php

Bernat Yarn
320 Livingstone Ave. South
Box 40
Listowel, ON
Canada N4W 3H3
888-368-8401

Berroco Inc.
1 Tupperware Dr., Suite 4
N. Smithfield, RI 02896
401-769-1212
http://berroco.com

Blue Sky Alpacas, Inc.
P.O. Box 88
Cedar, MN 55011
888-460-8862
www.blueskyalpacas.com

Brown Sheep Company, Inc.
100662 County Road 16
Mitchell, NE 69357
800-826-9136
www.brownsheep.com/index.htm

Caron International
P.O. Box 222
Washington, NC 27889
www.caron.com/index.html

Cascade Yarns
P.O. Box 58168
Tukwila, WA 98138
800-548-1048
www.cascadeyarns.com/index.asp

Cherry Tree Hill Yarn
100 Cherry Tree Hill Lane
Barton, VT 05822
802-525-3311
www.cherryyarn.com

Classic Elite Yarns
122 Western Avenue
Lowell, MA 01851-1434
978-453-2837
www.classiceliteyarns.com/home.php

Conjoined Creations
P.O. Box 4110
Cave Creek, AZ 85327
480-488-0324
www.conjoinedcreations.com

Debbie Bliss
Distributed by Knitting Fever Inc.
315 Bayview Avenue
Amityville, NY 11701
516-546-3600
www.debbieblissonline.com/yarns.asp

The Fibre Company
Distributed by Kelbourne Woolens
915 N. 28th Street, Second Floor
Philadelphia, PA 19130
215-687-5534
www.thefibreco.com

Harrisville Designs
P.O. Box 806
Harrisville, NH 03450
800-338-9415
www.harrisville.com

Karabella Yarns, Inc.
1201 Broadway
New York, NY 10001
800-550-0898
www.karabellayarns.com/default.aspx

Knit Picks
13118 N.E. 4th Street
Vancouver, WA 98684
800-574-1323
www.knitpicks.com/knitting.cfm

Knitting Fever, Inc.
P.O. Box 336
315 Bayview Avenue
Amityville, NY 11701
516-546-3600
www.knittingfever.com

Lion Brand Yarn
135 Kero Road
Carlstadt, NJ 07072
800-795-5466.
http://cache.lionbrand.com

Lorna's Laces Yarns
4229 North Honore St.
Chicago, IL 60613
773-935-3803
www.lornaslaces.net/home.asp

Muench Yarns, Inc.
1323 Scott Street
Petaluma, CA 94954-1135
800-733-9276
www.muenchyarns.com

Patons Yarn
320 Livingstone Avenue South
Box 40
Listowel, ON
Canada N4W 3H3
888-368-8401
www.patonsyarns.com

Red Heart Yarn
Consumer Services
P.O. Box 12229
Greenville, SC 29612-0229
800-648-1479
www.redheart.com

Rowan Yarns
Green Lane Mill
Holmfirth, West Yorkshire
HD9 2DX
England
01484-681881

Trendsetter Yarns
16745 Saticoy Street, Suite 101
Van Nuys, CA 91406
818-780-5497
www.trendsetteryarns.com/index.asp

Westminster Fibers
165 Ledge Street
Nashua, NH 03060
800-445-9276
www.westminsterfibers.com

Notions

Addi Needle Shop
c/o Bob and Nancy's Services
304 Tasman Place
Philomath, OR 97370
541-929-2359
www.addineedleshop.com

Clover Needlecraft, Inc.
1441 S Carlos Avenue
Ontario, CA 91761
800-233-1703
www.clover-usa.com

Lantern Moon
7911 N.E. 33rd Drive, Suite 140
Portland, OR 97211
800-530-4170
www.lanternmoon.com/products.asp

Tinsel Trading
1 West 37th Street
New York, NY 10018
212-730-1030
www.tinseltrading.com/index.php

ndex